# TEACHER'S PET PUBLICATIONS

PUZZLE PACK
for
Bless Me, Ultima

based on the book by
Rudolfo Anaya

Written by
William T. Collins

© 2005 Teacher's Pet Publications
All Rights Reserved

The materials in this packet are copyrighted
by Teacher's Pet Publications, Inc.

These pages may be duplicated by the purchaser
for use in the purchaser's own classroom.

Copying any of these materials and distributing them
for any other purpose is a violation of the copyright laws.

© 2005 Teacher's Pet Publications, Inc.
www.tpet.com

INTRODUCTION
If you already own the LitPlan for this title, this Puzzle Pack will refresh your Unit Resource Materials and Vocabulary Resource Materials sections plus give you additional materials you can substitute into the tests. If you do not already have a complete LitPlan, these pages will give you some supplemental materials to use with your own plan. There are two main groups of materials: one set for unit words (such as characters' names, symbols, places, etc.) and one set for vocabulary words associated with the book.

WORD LIST
There is a word list for both the unit words and the vocabulary words. These lists show you which words are being used in the materials and the clues or definitions being used for those words. You may want to give students a word list with clues/definitions to help them, or you may want students to only have a word list (without clues/definitions) if you want them to work a little harder. Both are available for duplication. The word lists can also be your "calling key" for the bingo games.

FILL IN THE BLANK AND MATCHING
There are 4 each of the fill in the blank and matching worksheets for both the unit and vocabulary words. These pages can be used either as extra worksheets for students or as objective parts of a unit test. They can be done individually if students need extra help or as a whole class activity to review the material covered.

MAGIC SQUARES
The magic squares not only reinforce the material covered but also work on reasoning and math skills. Many teachers have told us that their students really enjoy doing these!

WORD SEARCH PUZZLES
The word search words go in all directions, as indicated on your answer keys. Two of the word search puzzles have the clues listed rather than the words. This makes the puzzle a little more difficult, but it reinforces the material better. Two word search puzzles have words only for students who find the clue puzzles too difficult.

CROSSWORD PUZZLES
Both unit and vocabulary word sections have 4 crossword puzzles.

BINGO CARDS
There are 32 individual bingo cards for the unit words and 32 individual bingo cards for the vocabulary words. You can use your word list as a "call list," calling the words at random and marking them off of your list as you go, or you could use the flash cards by cutting them apart and drawing the words at random from a hat (or box or whatever). To make a better review, you might ask for the definition and spelling of each word as you call it out–or you could call out the definitions and have students tell you the words they need to look for on the puzzle.

JUGGLE LETTERS
The vocabulary juggle letter game is intended to help students learn the spellings of the words. One sheet has the definitions listed on it as an extra help for students who need it or to reinforce the definitions if you choose to do so.

FLASH CARDS
We've included a set of vocabulary flash cards you can duplicate, cut, and fold for your students. Some teachers make a few sets for general use by the class; others make a set for each student. Some teachers duplicate them for each student and have the students cut & fold their own. You can cut out just the words and put them in a hat, have each student pick out one word and write the definition and a sentence for that word. Students then swap words and papers, with the next student adding a sentence of his own under the last one. You can have students swap as many times as you like. Each time the student will read the sentences written prior to his own and then add a sentence. You can cut out the words and definitions separately and play "I Have; Who Has?" Each student in the room draws a word and definition. The first student says, "I have (the name of the word). Who has the definition?" The student with the definition reads it then says, "I have (the name of the vocabulary word she has). Who has the definition?" The round continues until all words and definitions have been given.

Bless Me Ultima Word List

No.	Word	Clue/Definition
1.	ANAYA	Author
2.	ANTONIO	In conflict about his destiny
3.	CARP	What the people were turned into
4.	CHAVEZ	Wanted revenge for his brother's murder
5.	CICO	Took Antonio to see the golden carp
6.	COMMUNION	Antonio expected to get answers from God after making it
7.	CROSS	What a witch couldn't stand to wear
8.	CURANDERA	Ultima's occupation
9.	DEBORAH	Well-mannered Marez daughter
10.	DROWNED	How Florence died
11.	EUGENE	Most forceful brother
12.	EYE	What owl took from Tenorio
13.	FLORENCE	Believed he had never sinned
14.	GOLDEN	Color of the god-carp
15.	GRANDE	Term of respect for Ultima: La ___
16.	GUADALUPE	Town where Marez family lived
17.	JASON	His Indian told the story about the carp
18.	JUNIPER	Tree where Narcisco died
19.	LONELINESS	What Antonio felt his first day at school
20.	LUCAS	Luna uncle cured by Ultima
21.	LUNA	Farming family
22.	LUPITO	War-crazed murderer
23.	MAESTAS	First grade teacher: Miss ___
24.	NARCISCO	Died trying to warn Ultima of danger
25.	OWL	Ultima's pet and spirit
26.	PASTURAS	Ultima's home before coming to the Marez home: Las ___
27.	PEDRO	Luna uncle who drove to warn Ultima
28.	PUERTO	Home of Maria's farming relatives: El ___ De La Luna
29.	SAMUEL	Told Antonio the story of the carp
30.	SPANISH	Antonio's native language
31.	TELLEZ	Believed his house was cursed
32.	TENORIO	Wanted revenge for his daughters' deaths
33.	THERESA	Coached in manners by her sister
34.	TREMENTINA	Tenorio's family name
35.	VAQUERO	Gabriel's preferred occupation
36.	VITAMIN	Always running: ___ Kid
37.	WAR	Where Marez boys were at the beginning of the novel
38.	WATER	What surrounded the town of Guadalupe
39.	WITCH	Ultima was accused of being one

Bless Me Ultima Fill In The Blank 1

_____ 1. His Indian told the story about the carp
_____ 2. Died trying to warn Ultima of danger
_____ 3. What the people were turned into
_____ 4. Tree where Narcisco died
_____ 5. Author
_____ 6. Coached in manners by her sister
_____ 7. What Antonio felt his first day at school
_____ 8. Home of Maria's farming relatives: El ___ De La Luna
_____ 9. Tenorio's family name
_____ 10. Antonio expected to get answers from God after making it
_____ 11. War-crazed murderer
_____ 12. What a witch couldn't stand to wear
_____ 13. Believed he had never sinned
_____ 14. Color of the god-carp
_____ 15. Believed his house was cursed
_____ 16. Always running: ___ Kid
_____ 17. In conflict about his destiny
_____ 18. Well-mannered Marez daughter
_____ 19. Luna uncle who drove to warn Ultima
_____ 20. Ultima's pet and spirit

Bless Me Ultima Fill In The Blank 1 Answer Key

JASON	1. His Indian told the story about the carp
NARCISO	2. Died trying to warn Ultima of danger
CARP	3. What the people were turned into
JUNIPER	4. Tree where Narciso died
ANAYA	5. Author
THERESA	6. Coached in manners by her sister
LONELINESS	7. What Antonio felt his first day at school
PUERTO	8. Home of Maria's farming relatives: El ___ De La Luna
TREMENTINA	9. Tenorio's family name
COMMUNION	10. Antonio expected to get answers from God after making it
LUPITO	11. War-crazed murderer
CROSS	12. What a witch couldn't stand to wear
FLORENCE	13. Believed he had never sinned
GOLDEN	14. Color of the god-carp
TELLEZ	15. Believed his house was cursed
VITAMIN	16. Always running: ___ Kid
ANTONIO	17. In conflict about his destiny
DEBORAH	18. Well-mannered Marez daughter
PEDRO	19. Luna uncle who drove to warn Ultima
OWL	20. Ultima's pet and spirit

Bless Me Ultima Fill In The Blank 2

_____ 1. What owl took from Tenorio
_____ 2. War-crazed murderer
_____ 3. Term of respect for Ultima: La ___
_____ 4. Tree where Narcisco died
_____ 5. Wanted revenge for his brother's murder
_____ 6. Believed his house was cursed
_____ 7. Author
_____ 8. Farming family
_____ 9. Took Antonio to see the golden carp
_____ 10. Luna uncle cured by Ultima
_____ 11. Home of Maria's farming relatives: El ___ De La Luna
_____ 12. Town where Marez family lived
_____ 13. What the people were turned into
_____ 14. Ultima's pet and spirit
_____ 15. Antonio expected to get answers from God after making it
_____ 16. Gabriel's preferred occupation
_____ 17. Ultima was accused of being one
_____ 18. What a witch couldn't stand to wear
_____ 19. Believed he had never sinned
_____ 20. Coached in manners by her sister

Bless Me Ultima Fill In The Blank 2 Answer Key

EYE	1. What owl took from Tenorio
LUPITO	2. War-crazed murderer
GRANDE	3. Term of respect for Ultima: La ___
JUNIPER	4. Tree where Narciso died
CHAVEZ	5. Wanted revenge for his brother's murder
TELLEZ	6. Believed his house was cursed
ANAYA	7. Author
LUNA	8. Farming family
CICO	9. Took Antonio to see the golden carp
LUCAS	10. Luna uncle cured by Ultima
PUERTO	11. Home of Maria's farming relatives: El ___ De La Luna
GUADALUPE	12. Town where Marez family lived
CARP	13. What the people were turned into
OWL	14. Ultima's pet and spirit
COMMUNION	15. Antonio expected to get answers from God after making it
VAQUERO	16. Gabriel's preferred occupation
WITCH	17. Ultima was accused of being one
CROSS	18. What a witch couldn't stand to wear
FLORENCE	19. Believed he had never sinned
THERESA	20. Coached in manners by her sister

Bless Me Ultima Fill In The Blank 3

_____ 1. Took Antonio to see the golden carp

_____ 2. Luna uncle cured by Ultima

_____ 3. Always running: ___ Kid

_____ 4. Tree where Narciso died

_____ 5. First grade teacher: Miss ___

_____ 6. Ultima's home before coming to the Marez home: Las ___

_____ 7. Ultima was accused of being one

_____ 8. Color of the god-carp

_____ 9. Most forceful brother

_____ 10. War-crazed murderer

_____ 11. Ultima's occupation

_____ 12. Author

_____ 13. How Florence died

_____ 14. Ultima's pet and spirit

_____ 15. Antonio's native language

_____ 16. Term of respect for Ultima: La ___

_____ 17. Wanted revenge for his brother's murder

_____ 18. Gabriel's preferred occupation

_____ 19. In conflict about his destiny

_____ 20. Died trying to warn Ultima of danger

Bless Me Ultima Fill In The Blank 3 Answer Key

Answer	Clue
CICO	1. Took Antonio to see the golden carp
LUCAS	2. Luna uncle cured by Ultima
VITAMIN	3. Always running: ___ Kid
JUNIPER	4. Tree where Narciso died
MAESTAS	5. First grade teacher: Miss ___
PASTURAS	6. Ultima's home before coming to the Marez home: Las ___
WITCH	7. Ultima was accused of being one
GOLDEN	8. Color of the god-carp
EUGENE	9. Most forceful brother
LUPITO	10. War-crazed murderer
CURANDERA	11. Ultima's occupation
ANAYA	12. Author
DROWNED	13. How Florence died
OWL	14. Ultima's pet and spirit
SPANISH	15. Antonio's native language
GRANDE	16. Term of respect for Ultima: La ___
CHAVEZ	17. Wanted revenge for his brother's murder
VAQUERO	18. Gabriel's preferred occupation
ANTONIO	19. In conflict about his destiny
NARCISCO	20. Died trying to warn Ultima of danger

Bless Me Ultima Fill In The Blank 4

_____ 1. Coached in manners by her sister

_____ 2. First grade teacher: Miss ___

_____ 3. Most forceful brother

_____ 4. Color of the god-carp

_____ 5. Town where Marez family lived

_____ 6. Gabriel's preferred occupation

_____ 7. Believed his house was cursed

_____ 8. Died trying to warn Ultima of danger

_____ 9. Believed he had never sinned

_____ 10. His Indian told the story about the carp

_____ 11. What surrounded the town of Guadalupe

_____ 12. Wanted revenge for his brother's murder

_____ 13. Farming family

_____ 14. What Antonio felt his first day at school

_____ 15. Antonio's native language

_____ 16. Home of Maria's farming relatives: El ___ De La Luna

_____ 17. Wanted revenge for his daughters' deaths

_____ 18. Took Antonio to see the golden carp

_____ 19. Always running: ___ Kid

_____ 20. Term of respect for Ultima: La ___

Bless Me Ultima Fill In The Blank 4 Answer Key

THERESA	1.	Coached in manners by her sister
MAESTAS	2.	First grade teacher: Miss ___
EUGENE	3.	Most forceful brother
GOLDEN	4.	Color of the god-carp
GUADALUPE	5.	Town where Marez family lived
VAQUERO	6.	Gabriel's preferred occupation
TELLEZ	7.	Believed his house was cursed
NARCISCO	8.	Died trying to warn Ultima of danger
FLORENCE	9.	Believed he had never sinned
JASON	10.	His Indian told the story about the carp
WATER	11.	What surrounded the town of Guadalupe
CHAVEZ	12.	Wanted revenge for his brother's murder
LUNA	13.	Farming family
LONELINESS	14.	What Antonio felt his first day at school
SPANISH	15.	Antonio's native language
PUERTO	16.	Home of Maria's farming relatives: El ___ De La Luna
TENORIO	17.	Wanted revenge for his daughters' deaths
CICO	18.	Took Antonio to see the golden carp
VITAMIN	19.	Always running: ___ Kid
GRANDE	20.	Term of respect for Ultima: La ___

Bless Me Ultima Matching 1

___ 1. CURANDERA	A. Ultima was accused of being one
___ 2. ANTONIO	B. Well-mannered Marez daughter
___ 3. GUADALUPE	C. In conflict about his destiny
___ 4. GOLDEN	D. His Indian told the story about the carp
___ 5. SPANISH	E. Wanted revenge for his daughters' deaths
___ 6. LUPITO	F. Gabriel's preferred occupation
___ 7. CICO	G. Ultima's pet and spirit
___ 8. THERESA	H. Town where Marez family lived
___ 9. PUERTO	I. Took Antonio to see the golden carp
___ 10. OWL	J. Always running: ___ Kid
___ 11. TENORIO	K. Antonio expected to get answers from God after making it
___ 12. GRANDE	L. Home of Maria's farming relatives: El ___ De La Luna
___ 13. LONELINESS	M. What Antonio felt his first day at school
___ 14. COMMUNION	N. Antonio's native language
___ 15. DEBORAH	O. Believed he had never sinned
___ 16. LUCAS	P. Luna uncle who drove to warn Ultima
___ 17. WITCH	Q. Where Marez boys were at the beginning of the novel
___ 18. WAR	R. Coached in manners by her sister
___ 19. VITAMIN	S. Luna uncle cured by Ultima
___ 20. VAQUERO	T. Ultima's occupation
___ 21. PEDRO	U. Color of the god-carp
___ 22. CARP	V. What the people were turned into
___ 23. FLORENCE	W. War-crazed murderer
___ 24. ANAYA	X. Term of respect for Ultima: La ___
___ 25. JASON	Y. Author

Bless Me Ultima Matching 1 Answer Key

T - 1. CURANDERA		A. Ultima was accused of being one
C - 2. ANTONIO		B. Well-mannered Marez daughter
H - 3. GUADALUPE		C. In conflict about his destiny
U - 4. GOLDEN		D. His Indian told the story about the carp
N - 5. SPANISH		E. Wanted revenge for his daughters' deaths
W - 6. LUPITO		F. Gabriel's preferred occupation
I - 7. CICO		G. Ultima's pet and spirit
R - 8. THERESA		H. Town where Marez family lived
L - 9. PUERTO		I. Took Antonio to see the golden carp
G - 10. OWL		J. Always running: ___ Kid
E - 11. TENORIO		K. Antonio expected to get answers from God after making it
X - 12. GRANDE		L. Home of Maria's farming relatives: El ___ De La Luna
M - 13. LONELINESS		M. What Antonio felt his first day at school
K - 14. COMMUNION		N. Antonio's native language
B - 15. DEBORAH		O. Believed he had never sinned
S - 16. LUCAS		P. Luna uncle who drove to warn Ultima
A - 17. WITCH		Q. Where Marez boys were at the beginning of the novel
Q - 18. WAR		R. Coached in manners by her sister
J - 19. VITAMIN		S. Luna uncle cured by Ultima
F - 20. VAQUERO		T. Ultima's occupation
P - 21. PEDRO		U. Color of the god-carp
V - 22. CARP		V. What the people were turned into
O - 23. FLORENCE		W. War-crazed murderer
Y - 24. ANAYA		X. Term of respect for Ultima: La ___
D - 25. JASON		Y. Author

Bless Me Ultima Matching 2

___ 1. LUCAS   A. Luna uncle cured by Ultima
___ 2. LUNA   B. Told Antonio the story of the carp
___ 3. CICO   C. Term of respect for Ultima: La ___
___ 4. PUERTO   D. Home of Maria's farming relatives: El ___ De La Luna
___ 5. TELLEZ   E. Tenorio's family name
___ 6. GRANDE   F. Most forceful brother
___ 7. OWL   G. Town where Marez family lived
___ 8. SPANISH   H. What a witch couldn't stand to wear
___ 9. JASON   I. Coached in manners by her sister
___ 10. EUGENE   J. Took Antonio to see the golden carp
___ 11. ANTONIO   K. Well-mannered Marez daughter
___ 12. CROSS   L. Wanted revenge for his brother's murder
___ 13. DEBORAH   M. Color of the god-carp
___ 14. COMMUNION   N. What owl took from Tenorio
___ 15. JUNIPER   O. In conflict about his destiny
___ 16. GOLDEN   P. Tree where Narciso died
___ 17. PASTURAS   Q. Ultima's home before coming to the Marez home: Las ___
___ 18. WATER   R. Antonio expected to get answers from God after making it
___ 19. EYE   S. Farming family
___ 20. SAMUEL   T. His Indian told the story about the carp
___ 21. CHAVEZ   U. How Florence died
___ 22. TREMENTINA   V. What surrounded the town of Guadalupe
___ 23. THERESA   W. Ultima's pet and spirit
___ 24. DROWNED   X. Antonio's native language
___ 25. GUADALUPE   Y. Believed his house was cursed

Bless Me Ultima Matching 2 Answer Key

A - 1. LUCAS	A.	Luna uncle cured by Ultima
S - 2. LUNA	B.	Told Antonio the story of the carp
J - 3. CICO	C.	Term of respect for Ultima: La ___
D - 4. PUERTO	D.	Home of Maria's farming relatives: El ___ De La Luna
Y - 5. TELLEZ	E.	Tenorio's family name
C - 6. GRANDE	F.	Most forceful brother
W - 7. OWL	G.	Town where Marez family lived
X - 8. SPANISH	H.	What a witch couldn't stand to wear
T - 9. JASON	I.	Coached in manners by her sister
F - 10. EUGENE	J.	Took Antonio to see the golden carp
O - 11. ANTONIO	K.	Well-mannered Marez daughter
H - 12. CROSS	L.	Wanted revenge for his brother's murder
K - 13. DEBORAH	M.	Color of the god-carp
R - 14. COMMUNION	N.	What owl took from Tenorio
P - 15. JUNIPER	O.	In conflict about his destiny
M - 16. GOLDEN	P.	Tree where Narciso died
Q - 17. PASTURAS	Q.	Ultima's home before coming to the Marez home: Las ___
V - 18. WATER	R.	Antonio expected to get answers from God after making it
N - 19. EYE	S.	Farming family
B - 20. SAMUEL	T.	His Indian told the story about the carp
L - 21. CHAVEZ	U.	How Florence died
E - 22. TREMENTINA	V.	What surrounded the town of Guadalupe
I - 23. THERESA	W.	Ultima's pet and spirit
U - 24. DROWNED	X.	Antonio's native language
G - 25. GUADALUPE	Y.	Believed his house was cursed

Bless Me Ultima Matching 3

___ 1. LUCAS   A. Luna uncle who drove to warn Ultima
___ 2. EUGENE   B. What owl took from Tenorio
___ 3. CICO   C. Gabriel's preferred occupation
___ 4. NARCISCO   D. Tenorio's family name
___ 5. VITAMIN   E. Most forceful brother
___ 6. JUNIPER   F. In conflict about his destiny
___ 7. CHAVEZ   G. Wanted revenge for his daughters' deaths
___ 8. CROSS   H. Color of the god-carp
___ 9. VAQUERO   I. Died trying to warn Ultima of danger
___10. COMMUNION   J. Author
___11. PASTURAS   K. War-crazed murderer
___12. TREMENTINA   L. Antonio's native language
___13. LUNA   M. Wanted revenge for his brother's murder
___14. PEDRO   N. Farming family
___15. WATER   O. What a witch couldn't stand to wear
___16. ANAYA   P. Tree where Narcisco died
___17. LUPITO   Q. Antonio expected to get answers from God after making it
___18. DEBORAH   R. Well-mannered Marez daughter
___19. GOLDEN   S. Ultima's home before coming to the Marez home: Las ___
___20. ANTONIO   T. Luna uncle cured by Ultima
___21. JASON   U. Always running: ___ Kid
___22. TENORIO   V. What surrounded the town of Guadalupe
___23. TELLEZ   W. Believed his house was cursed
___24. SPANISH   X. Took Antonio to see the golden carp
___25. EYE   Y. His Indian told the story about the carp

Bless Me Ultima Matching 3 Answer Key

T - 1. LUCAS	A.	Luna uncle who drove to warn Ultima
E - 2. EUGENE	B.	What owl took from Tenorio
X - 3. CICO	C.	Gabriel's preferred occupation
I - 4. NARCISCO	D.	Tenorio's family name
U - 5. VITAMIN	E.	Most forceful brother
P - 6. JUNIPER	F.	In conflict about his destiny
M - 7. CHAVEZ	G.	Wanted revenge for his daughters' deaths
O - 8. CROSS	H.	Color of the god-carp
C - 9. VAQUERO	I.	Died trying to warn Ultima of danger
Q - 10. COMMUNION	J.	Author
S - 11. PASTURAS	K.	War-crazed murderer
D - 12. TREMENTINA	L.	Antonio's native language
N - 13. LUNA	M.	Wanted revenge for his brother's murder
A - 14. PEDRO	N.	Farming family
V - 15. WATER	O.	What a witch couldn't stand to wear
J - 16. ANAYA	P.	Tree where Narcisco died
K - 17. LUPITO	Q.	Antonio expected to get answers from God after making it
R - 18. DEBORAH	R.	Well-mannered Marez daughter
H - 19. GOLDEN	S.	Ultima's home before coming to the Marez home: Las ___
F - 20. ANTONIO	T.	Luna uncle cured by Ultima
Y - 21. JASON	U.	Always running: ___ Kid
G - 22. TENORIO	V.	What surrounded the town of Guadalupe
W - 23. TELLEZ	W.	Believed his house was cursed
L - 24. SPANISH	X.	Took Antonio to see the golden carp
B - 25. EYE	Y.	His Indian told the story about the carp

Bless Me Ultima Matching 4

___ 1. JUNIPER	A. War-crazed murderer
___ 2. WITCH	B. Antonio's native language
___ 3. SAMUEL	C. Gabriel's preferred occupation
___ 4. VAQUERO	D. Wanted revenge for his brother's murder
___ 5. EUGENE	E. Luna uncle who drove to warn Ultima
___ 6. CHAVEZ	F. Luna uncle cured by Ultima
___ 7. SPANISH	G. Ultima was accused of being one
___ 8. PASTURAS	H. Wanted revenge for his daughters' deaths
___ 9. TREMENTINA	I. Author
___ 10. GUADALUPE	J. Ultima's home before coming to the Marez home: Las ___
___ 11. NARCISCO	K. Home of Maria's farming relatives: El ___ De La Luna
___ 12. DEBORAH	L. Town where Marez family lived
___ 13. LUCAS	M. Most forceful brother
___ 14. FLORENCE	N. Coached in manners by her sister
___ 15. MAESTAS	O. Died trying to warn Ultima of danger
___ 16. PEDRO	P. Tree where Narcisco died
___ 17. LUPITO	Q. Tenorio's family name
___ 18. ANAYA	R. First grade teacher: Miss ___
___ 19. TENORIO	S. How Florence died
___ 20. LUNA	T. Well-mannered Marez daughter
___ 21. PUERTO	U. Farming family
___ 22. WATER	V. Believed he had never sinned
___ 23. THERESA	W. What surrounded the town of Guadalupe
___ 24. CARP	X. What the people were turned into
___ 25. DROWNED	Y. Told Antonio the story of the carp

Bless Me Ultima Matching 4 Answer Key

P - 1. JUNIPER	A.	War-crazed murderer
G - 2. WITCH	B.	Antonio's native language
Y - 3. SAMUEL	C.	Gabriel's preferred occupation
C - 4. VAQUERO	D.	Wanted revenge for his brother's murder
M - 5. EUGENE	E.	Luna uncle who drove to warn Ultima
D - 6. CHAVEZ	F.	Luna uncle cured by Ultima
B - 7. SPANISH	G.	Ultima was accused of being one
J - 8. PASTURAS	H.	Wanted revenge for his daughters' deaths
Q - 9. TREMENTINA	I.	Author
L - 10. GUADALUPE	J.	Ultima's home before coming to the Marez home: Las ___
O - 11. NARCISCO	K.	Home of Maria's farming relatives: El ___ De La Luna
T - 12. DEBORAH	L.	Town where Marez family lived
F - 13. LUCAS	M.	Most forceful brother
V - 14. FLORENCE	N.	Coached in manners by her sister
R - 15. MAESTAS	O.	Died trying to warn Ultima of danger
E - 16. PEDRO	P.	Tree where Narcisco died
A - 17. LUPITO	Q.	Tenorio's family name
I - 18. ANAYA	R.	First grade teacher: Miss ___
H - 19. TENORIO	S.	How Florence died
U - 20. LUNA	T.	Well-mannered Marez daughter
K - 21. PUERTO	U.	Farming family
W - 22. WATER	V.	Believed he had never sinned
N - 23. THERESA	W.	What surrounded the town of Guadalupe
X - 24. CARP	X.	What the people were turned into
S - 25. DROWNED	Y.	Told Antonio the story of the carp

Bless Me Ultima Magic Squares 1

Match the definition with the vocabulary word. Put your answers in the magic squares below. When your answers are correct, all columns and rows will add to the same number.

A. LONELINESS E. ANTONIO   I. DROWNED   M. OWL
B. LUNA   F. EYE   J. VAQUERO   N. CHAVEZ
C. ANAYA   G. FLORENCE   K. NARCISCO   O. PEDRO
D. DEBORAH   H. THERESA   L. TREMENTINA   P. COMMUNION

1. Ultima's pet and spirit
2. What owl took from Tenorio
3. Coached in manners by her sister
4. Luna uncle who drove to warn Ultima
5. Tenorio's family name
6. Author
7. What Antonio felt his first day at school
8. Gabriel's preferred occupation
9. Died trying to warn Ultima of danger
10. Well-mannered Marez daughter
11. Farming family
12. How Florence died
13. Wanted revenge for his brother's murder
14. In conflict about his destiny
15. Believed he had never sinned
16. Antonio expected to get answers from God after making it

A=	B=	C=	D=
E=	F=	G=	H=
I=	J=	K=	L=
M=	N=	O=	P=

Bless Me Ultima Magic Squares 1 Answer Key

Match the definition with the vocabulary word. Put your answers in the magic squares below. When your answers are correct, all columns and rows will add to the same number.

A. LONELINESS E. ANTONIO   I. DROWNED   M. OWL
B. LUNA   F. EYE   J. VAQUERO   N. CHAVEZ
C. ANAYA   G. FLORENCE   K. NARCISCO   O. PEDRO
D. DEBORAH   H. THERESA   L. TREMENTINA P. COMMUNION

1. Ultima's pet and spirit
2. What owl took from Tenorio
3. Coached in manners by her sister
4. Luna uncle who drove to warn Ultima
5. Tenorio's family name
6. Author
7. What Antonio felt his first day at school
8. Gabriel's preferred occupation
9. Died trying to warn Ultima of danger
10. Well-mannered Marez daughter
11. Farming family
12. How Florence died
13. Wanted revenge for his brother's murder
14. In conflict about his destiny
15. Believed he had never sinned
16. Antonio expected to get answers from God after making it

A=7	B=11	C=6	D=10
E=14	F=2	G=15	H=3
I=12	J=8	K=9	L=5
M=1	N=13	O=4	P=16

Bless Me Ultima Magic Squares 2

Match the definition with the vocabulary word. Put your answers in the magic squares below. When your answers are correct, all columns and rows will add to the same number.

A. ANTONIO   E. PEDRO   I. TENORIO   M. OWL
B. NARCISCO   F. FLORENCE   J. JASON   N. LONELINESS
C. LUPITO   G. TREMENTINA   K. SPANISH   O. THERESA
D. WATER   H. EUGENE   L. EYE   P. MAESTAS

1. Coached in manners by her sister
2. What surrounded the town of Guadalupe
3. His Indian told the story about the carp
4. Luna uncle who drove to warn Ultima
5. Wanted revenge for his daughters' deaths
6. Believed he had never sinned
7. First grade teacher: Miss ___
8. War-crazed murderer
9. Most forceful brother
10. Antonio's native language
11. In conflict about his destiny
12. What Antonio felt his first day at school
13. Died trying to warn Ultima of danger
14. Ultima's pet and spirit
15. Tenorio's family name
16. What owl took from Tenorio

A=	B=	C=	D=
E=	F=	G=	H=
I=	J=	K=	L=
M=	N=	O=	P=

Bless Me Ultima Magic Squares 2 Answer Key

Match the definition with the vocabulary word. Put your answers in the magic squares below. When your answers are correct, all columns and rows will add to the same number.

A. ANTONIO   E. PEDRO   I. TENORIO   M. OWL
B. NARCISCO   F. FLORENCE   J. JASON   N. LONELINESS
C. LUPITO   G. TREMENTINA   K. SPANISH   O. THERESA
D. WATER   H. EUGENE   L. EYE   P. MAESTAS

1. Coached in manners by her sister
2. What surrounded the town of Guadalupe
3. His Indian told the story about the carp
4. Luna uncle who drove to warn Ultima
5. Wanted revenge for his daughters' deaths
6. Believed he had never sinned
7. First grade teacher: Miss ___
8. War-crazed murderer
9. Most forceful brother
10. Antonio's native language
11. In conflict about his destiny
12. What Antonio felt his first day at school
13. Died trying to warn Ultima of danger
14. Ultima's pet and spirit
15. Tenorio's family name
16. What owl took from Tenorio

A=11	B=13	C=8	D=2
E=4	F=6	G=15	H=9
I=5	J=3	K=10	L=16
M=14	N=12	O=1	P=7

Bless Me Ultima Magic Squares 3

Match the definition with the vocabulary word. Put your answers in the magic squares below. When your answers are correct, all columns and rows will add to the same number.

A. GUADALUPE
B. VITAMIN
C. TREMENTINA
D. DROWNED
E. PUERTO
F. SPANISH
G. GOLDEN
H. TENORIO
I. JASON
J. DEBORAH
K. OWL
L. LUNA
M. SAMUEL
N. WITCH
O. ANTONIO
P. CHAVEZ

1. Ultima was accused of being one
2. Color of the god-carp
3. Farming family
4. Town where Marez family lived
5. Ultima's pet and spirit
6. Always running: ___ Kid
7. Told Antonio the story of the carp
8. Wanted revenge for his daughters' deaths
9. Home of Maria's farming relatives: El ___ De La Luna
10. Wanted revenge for his brother's murder
11. Tenorio's family name
12. Well-mannered Marez daughter
13. How Florence died
14. His Indian told the story about the carp
15. Antonio's native language
16. In conflict about his destiny

A=	B=	C=	D=
E=	F=	G=	H=
I=	J=	K=	L=
M=	N=	O=	P=

Bless Me Ultima Magic Squares 3 Answer Key

Match the definition with the vocabulary word. Put your answers in the magic squares below. When your answers are correct, all columns and rows will add to the same number.

A. GUADALUPE   E. PUERTO   I. JASON   M. SAMUEL
B. VITAMIN   F. SPANISH   J. DEBORAH   N. WITCH
C. TREMENTINA G. GOLDEN   K. OWL   O. ANTONIO
D. DROWNED   H. TENORIO   L. LUNA   P. CHAVEZ

1. Ultima was accused of being one
2. Color of the god-carp
3. Farming family
4. Town where Marez family lived
5. Ultima's pet and spirit
6. Always running: ___ Kid
7. Told Antonio the story of the carp
8. Wanted revenge for his daughters' deaths
9. Home of Maria's farming relatives: El ___ De La Luna
10. Wanted revenge for his brother's murder
11. Tenorio's family name
12. Well-mannered Marez daughter
13. How Florence died
14. His Indian told the story about the carp
15. Antonio's native language
16. In conflict about his destiny

A=4	B=6	C=11	D=13
E=9	F=15	G=2	H=8
I=14	J=12	K=5	L=3
M=7	N=1	O=16	P=10

26
Copyrighted

Bless Me Ultima Magic Squares 4

Match the definition with the vocabulary word. Put your answers in the magic squares below. When your answers are correct, all columns and rows will add to the same number.

A. NARCISCO   E. TENORIO   I. CARP   M. SPANISH
B. WATER   F. LUNA   J. COMMUNION   N. OWL
C. LONELINESS G. ANTONIO   K. JUNIPER   O. WITCH
D. THERESA   H. GRANDE   L. PUERTO   P. ANAYA

1. Farming family
2. What the people were turned into
3. Ultima was accused of being one
4. Coached in manners by her sister
5. Antonio's native language
6. What surrounded the town of Guadalupe
7. Term of respect for Ultima: La ___
8. Tree where Narcisco died
9. What Antonio felt his first day at school
10. Author
11. Antonio expected to get answers from God after making it
12. Wanted revenge for his daughters' deaths
13. Home of Maria's farming relatives: El ___ De La Luna
14. In conflict about his destiny
15. Died trying to warn Ultima of danger
16. Ultima's pet and spirit

A=	B=	C=	D=
E=	F=	G=	H=
I=	J=	K=	L=
M=	N=	O=	P=

Bless Me Ultima Magic Squares 4 Answer Key

Match the definition with the vocabulary word. Put your answers in the magic squares below. When your answers are correct, all columns and rows will add to the same number.

A. NARCISCO E. TENORIO I. CARP M. SPANISH
B. WATER F. LUNA J. COMMUNION N. OWL
C. LONELINESS G. ANTONIO K. JUNIPER O. WITCH
D. THERESA H. GRANDE L. PUERTO P. ANAYA

1. Farming family
2. What the people were turned into
3. Ultima was accused of being one
4. Coached in manners by her sister
5. Antonio's native language
6. What surrounded the town of Guadalupe
7. Term of respect for Ultima: La ___
8. Tree where Narcisco died
9. What Antonio felt his first day at school
10. Author
11. Antonio expected to get answers from God after making it
12. Wanted revenge for his daughters' deaths
13. Home of Maria's farming relatives: El ___ De La Luna
14. In conflict about his destiny
15. Died trying to warn Ultima of danger
16. Ultima's pet and spirit

A=15	B=6	C=9	D=4
E=12	F=1	G=14	H=7
I=2	J=11	K=8	L=13
M=5	N=16	O=3	P=10

Bless Me Ultima Word Search 1

```
C H A V E Z R M V X C K P C P H Y H Q Y
S F W N F V S B A R Y U T Y V E V Q P Z
P L K K D S A M U E L X R F F R D H X C
X O B H A B G S Y T S R W A A E R R S K
D R R Y Z J T E D A Z T Y W N C V W O L
A E A Z L E V F R W C T A W A D R T W C
X N O I N U M M O C W R O S R L E O P M
A C T O Q W C C T H Y R E B P H U R S W
J E R O Y E S A L R D R L L C A A N A S
S I R S N I M J S P E V D E U C N Z A Q
O T T E C I N A X H Q M D E L P E I G M
W B G R H I O S T J G N E B B L I K S W
V U A Q M S N O S B A W P N L O N T O H
E N V A W K K N P R J I M E T E R C O R
M O T R E U P S G V C T T V D I I A T T
C I P A S T U R A S H C Z L Q C N R H S
V L O N E L I N E S S H O W P D J A Q P
V A Q U E R O P G X Z G J U N I P E R S
```

Always running: ___ Kid (7)
Antonio expected to get answers from God after making it (9)
Antonio's native language (7)
Author (5)
Believed he had never sinned (8)
Believed his house was cursed (6)
Coached in manners by her sister (7)
Color of the god-carp (6)
Died trying to warn Ultima of danger (8)
Farming family (4)
First grade teacher: Miss ___ (7)
Gabriel's preferred occupation (7)
His Indian told the story about the carp (5)
Home of Maria's farming relatives: El ___ De La Luna (6)
How Florence died (7)
In conflict about his destiny (7)
Luna uncle cured by Ultima (5)
Luna uncle who drove to warn Ultima (5)
Most forceful brother (6)
Tenorio's family name (10)
Term of respect for Ultima: La ___ (6)
Told Antonio the story of the carp (6)
Took Antonio to see the golden carp (4)
Tree where Narcisco died (7)
Ultima was accused of being one (5)
Ultima's home before coming to the Marez home: Las ___ (8)
Ultima's occupation (9)
Ultima's pet and spirit (3)
Wanted revenge for his brother's murder (6)
Wanted revenge for his daughters' deaths (7)
War-crazed murderer (6)
Well-mannered Marez daughter (7)
What Antonio felt his first day at school (10)
What a witch couldn't stand to wear (5)
What owl took from Tenorio (3)
What surrounded the town of Guadalupe (5)
What the people were turned into (4)
Where Marez boys were at the beginning of the novel (3)

Bless Me Ultima Word Search 1 Answer Key

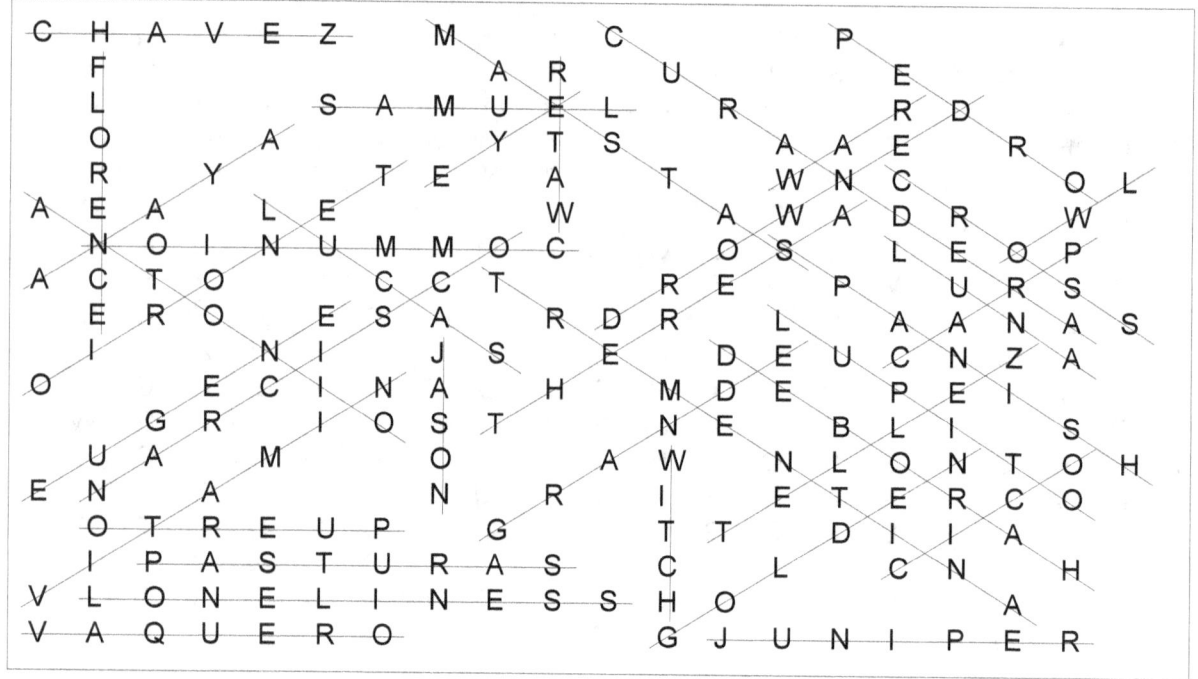

Always running: ___ Kid (7)
Antonio expected to get answers from God after making it (9)
Antonio's native language (7)
Author (5)
Believed he had never sinned (8)
Believed his house was cursed (6)
Coached in manners by her sister (7)
Color of the god-carp (6)
Died trying to warn Ultima of danger (8)
Farming family (4)
First grade teacher: Miss ___ (7)
Gabriel's preferred occupation (7)
His Indian told the story about the carp (5)
Home of Maria's farming relatives: El ___ De La Luna (6)
How Florence died (7)
In conflict about his destiny (7)
Luna uncle cured by Ultima (5)
Luna uncle who drove to warn Ultima (5)
Most forceful brother (6)
Tenorio's family name (10)
Term of respect for Ultima: La ___ (6)
Told Antonio the story of the carp (6)
Took Antonio to see the golden carp (4)
Tree where Narcisco died (7)
Ultima was accused of being one (5)
Ultima's home before coming to the Marez home: Las ___ (8)
Ultima's occupation (9)
Ultima's pet and spirit (3)
Wanted revenge for his brother's murder (6)
Wanted revenge for his daughters' deaths (7)
War-crazed murderer (6)
Well-mannered Marez daughter (7)
What Antonio felt his first day at school (10)
What a witch couldn't stand to wear (5)
What owl took from Tenorio (3)
What surrounded the town of Guadalupe (5)
What the people were turned into (4)
Where Marez boys were at the beginning of the novel (3)

Bless Me Ultima Word Search 2

```
F L O R E N C E A N T O N I O X V V R B
G U U G U A D A L U P E K L S W P V S C
S C J N D Z F D R J V P T F M A G C C Y
S A B G A C S Z Y P A L S H Q T M D J K
E S Y J H M H R R S T S P N E E Y U S Z
N L M U J N J F T F L W O H A R O B E D
I R R N J H G U H M C T R N A W E L L L
L T N I L G R D R R R D E W V J L S D P
E K R P P A T C O E T R U K I E X C A J
N M A E S T A S U B F O Q O T I P U L F
O A D R M G S P S V Y W A I A B D R C F
L R R G H E R W P K M N V R M V K A I Z
O L R C V T N A A E W E S O I X E N C R
Q M T W I E C T N Z U D N N N Y A D O B
G I J D D S J F I D P G Q E E Y M E C S
W D Q L P B C D S N E R E T A L F R S C
N L O N Z V Q O H R A B V N L L B A F S
K G C O M M U N I O N L A Z E V A H C W
```

Always running: ___ Kid (7)
Antonio expected to get answers from God after making it (9)
Antonio's native language (7)
Author (5)
Believed he had never sinned (8)
Believed his house was cursed (6)
Coached in manners by her sister (7)
Color of the god-carp (6)
Died trying to warn Ultima of danger (8)
Farming family (4)
First grade teacher: Miss ___ (7)
Gabriel's preferred occupation (7)
His Indian told the story about the carp (5)
Home of Maria's farming relatives: El ___ De La Luna (6)
How Florence died (7)
In conflict about his destiny (7)
Luna uncle cured by Ultima (5)
Luna uncle who drove to warn Ultima (5)
Most forceful brother (6)
Tenorio's family name (10)
Term of respect for Ultima: La ___ (6)
Told Antonio the story of the carp (6)
Took Antonio to see the golden carp (4)
Town where Marez family lived (9)
Tree where Narcisco died (7)
Ultima was accused of being one (5)
Ultima's home before coming to the Marez home: Las ___ (8)
Ultima's occupation (9)
Ultima's pet and spirit (3)
Wanted revenge for his brother's murder (6)
Wanted revenge for his daughters' deaths (7)
War-crazed murderer (6)
Well-mannered Marez daughter (7)
What Antonio felt his first day at school (10)
What a witch couldn't stand to wear (5)
What owl took from Tenorio (3)
What surrounded the town of Guadalupe (5)
What the people were turned into (4)
Where Marez boys were at the beginning of the novel (3)

Bless Me Ultima Word Search 2 Answer Key

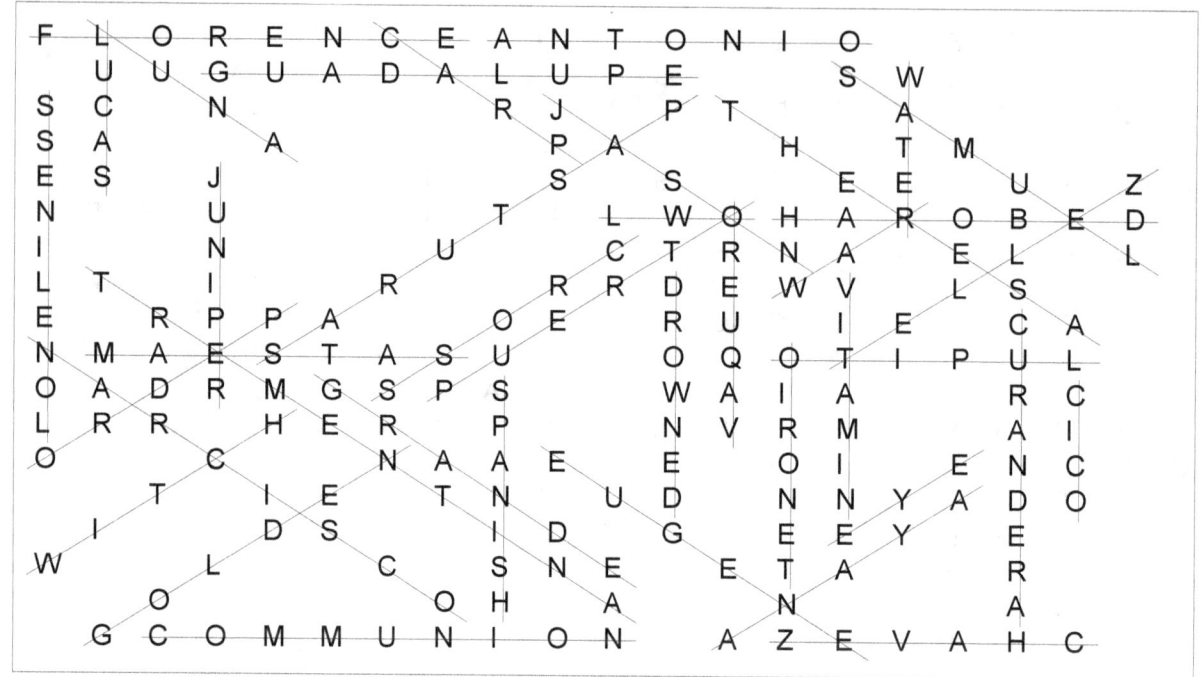

Always running: ___ Kid (7)
Antonio expected to get answers from God after making it (9)
Antonio's native language (7)
Author (5)
Believed he had never sinned (8)
Believed his house was cursed (6)
Coached in manners by her sister (7)
Color of the god-carp (6)
Died trying to warn Ultima of danger (8)
Farming family (4)
First grade teacher: Miss ___ (7)
Gabriel's preferred occupation (7)
His Indian told the story about the carp (5)
Home of Maria's farming relatives: El ___ De La Luna (6)
How Florence died (7)
In conflict about his destiny (7)
Luna uncle cured by Ultima (5)
Luna uncle who drove to warn Ultima (5)
Most forceful brother (6)
Tenorio's family name (10)
Term of respect for Ultima: La ___ (6)
Told Antonio the story of the carp (6)
Took Antonio to see the golden carp (4)
Town where Marez family lived (9)
Tree where Narcisco died (7)
Ultima was accused of being one (5)
Ultima's home before coming to the Marez home: Las ___ (8)
Ultima's occupation (9)
Ultima's pet and spirit (3)
Wanted revenge for his brother's murder (6)
Wanted revenge for his daughters' deaths (7)
War-crazed murderer (6)
Well-mannered Marez daughter (7)
What Antonio felt his first day at school (10)
What a witch couldn't stand to wear (5)
What owl took from Tenorio (3)
What surrounded the town of Guadalupe (5)
What the people were turned into (4)
Where Marez boys were at the beginning of the novel (3)

Bless Me Ultima Word Search 3

```
S P A N I S H G K H N W V Z S X H M R X
S A M U E L C H A V E Z E Z O C K W Q H
S X W F L O N H L S D L R W C T A A Y E
S A R U T S A P O W L J U N I P E R Y P
M K S R E R S N P E O U O C C T O E P F
D T E Q N N E V T G G S P S A B C B R M
D U K A O L R M T O A F R I E S Z H A B
P R N L R R E J E J N L L D T G X Y C T
P U O P I L H R D N G I C O J O A S U L
L E T W O Y T G N Y T U O N R N G S R S
D M D W N M V K A O J I A T A E Z O A T
V V P R R E A P R H P R N D G J N R N D
P I M E O H D E G F C Q L A A K C C D N
N T T N J R U R S I D P M P L L N R E F
P A F G F Q L P S T E U G E N E U X R W
W M B J A J K C Q V A Q B T D T K P A K
B I N V Z M O H D Y Z S S P H D Q R E R
J N L O N E L I N E S S J X W P P Y Z Q
```

ANAYA	DROWNED	JUNIPER	PASTURAS	TREMENTINA
ANTONIO	EUGENE	LONELINESS	PEDRO	VAQUERO
CARP	EYE	LUCAS	PUERTO	VITAMIN
CHAVEZ	FLORENCE	LUNA	SAMUEL	WAR
CICO	GOLDEN	LUPITO	SPANISH	WATER
CROSS	GRANDE	MAESTAS	TELLEZ	WITCH
CURANDERA	GUADALUPE	NARCISCO	TENORIO	
DEBORAH	JASON	OWL	THERESA	

Bless Me Ultima Word Search 3 Answer Key

ANAYA	DROWNED	JUNIPER	PASTURAS	TREMENTINA
ANTONIO	EUGENE	LONELINESS	PEDRO	VAQUERO
CARP	EYE	LUCAS	PUERTO	VITAMIN
CHAVEZ	FLORENCE	LUNA	SAMUEL	WAR
CICO	GOLDEN	LUPITO	SPANISH	WATER
CROSS	GRANDE	MAESTAS	TELLEZ	WITCH
CURANDERA	GUADALUPE	NARCISO	TENORIO	
DEBORAH	JASON	OWL	THERESA	

Bless Me Ultima Word Search 4

```
L P N L P G S C U R A N D E R A H W S T
U S W X C A P P C O M M U N I O N A Z J
P O M M A E S T A S S P P M G X C J D P
I V W C F M S T D N J H Q A T U H B Y V
T J A S O N E B U M I S M N L S R V A G
O M D D C Z N V L R N S X T T F T Q R V
T J G E W B I J H H A V H O M Y U H F P
Q H D B L O L T E B R S J N Z E Z G X S
D Y E O T U E C L V C O Z I R F R N H P
H T D R O W N E D C I C O O M Z L N A C
L B E A E E O A D R S T Y Z E M E C N F
M U V H R S L X O J C R A L Z D U R A X
P R R O G O A N Y J O W L M L Y M O Y W
P A L W R Q E N E G U E I O I M A S A J
W F Z D A T P S H Y T C G T Q N S S L Q
C D E A N I T N E M E R T Y C K D S M D
W P Q Z D W A T E R C A R P C H A V E Z
B S R S E P U L A D A U G J U N I P E R
```

ANAYA	DEBORAH	JASON	OWL	THERESA
ANTONIO	DROWNED	JUNIPER	PASTURAS	TREMENTINA
CARP	EUGENE	LONELINESS	PEDRO	VAQUERO
CHAVEZ	EYE	LUCAS	PUERTO	VITAMIN
CICO	FLORENCE	LUNA	SAMUEL	WAR
COMMUNION	GOLDEN	LUPITO	SPANISH	WATER
CROSS	GRANDE	MAESTAS	TELLEZ	WITCH
CURANDERA	GUADALUPE	NARCISCO	TENORIO	

Bless Me Ultima Word Search 4 Answer Key

```
L       L   P   S C U R A N D E R A           S
    W       A   P C O M M U N I O N A
U O     M A E S T A S         A             C
P           S T   N           N             U
I   J A S O N E   U R I       T             Q   V
T O         D     N   N S     O             U   A
T           E     I   R       N             E
    H       B L O R   S       I
        E   O T U E C   V C   O     Z   L   N   A
      D R O W N E D   I C O   O     E   E   C   N
      E A E E O A   R S T     E     D   C   R   A
  U   P R H R S L   O   C     L     U   R   O   Y
P   R O   O G O A N     O W L M     M   O   S   A
  A L     R   E N E G U E I O I     A   S   S
W F       D A T       Y T   G T     N   S   S
      E A N I T N E M E R T     C
    P       D W A T E R C A R P C H A V E Z
            E P U L A D A U G J U N I P E R
```

ANAYA   DEBORAH   JASON   OWL   THERESA

ANTONIO   DROWNED   JUNIPER   PASTURAS   TREMENTINA

CARP   EUGENE   LONELINESS   PEDRO   VAQUERO

CHAVEZ   EYE   LUCAS   PUERTO   VITAMIN

CICO   FLORENCE   LUNA   SAMUEL   WAR

COMMUNION   GOLDEN   LUPITO   SPANISH   WATER

CROSS   GRANDE   MAESTAS   TELLEZ   WITCH

CURANDERA   GUADALUPE   NARCISCO   TENORIO

Bless Me Ultima Crossword 1

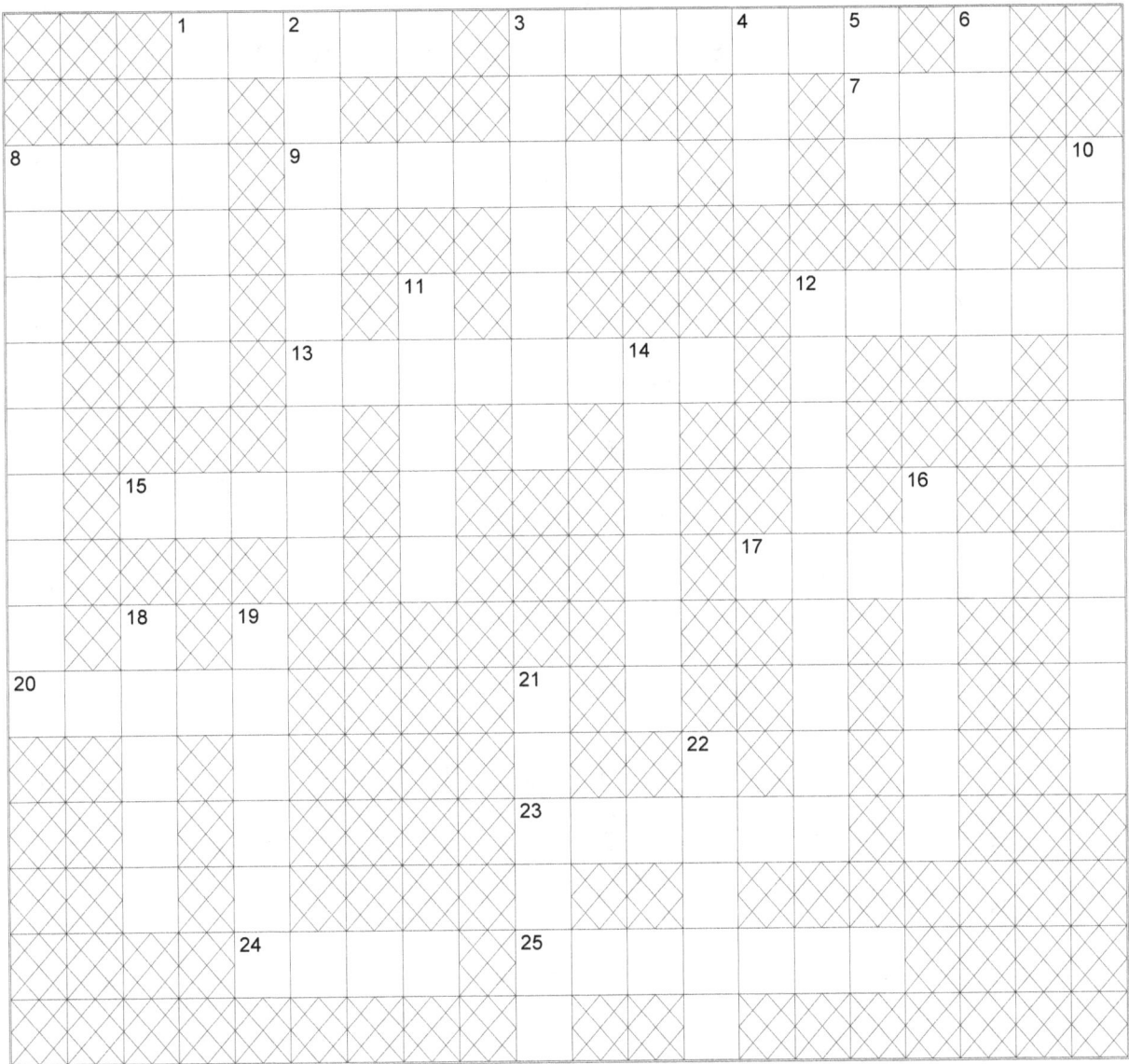

Across
1. Luna uncle cured by Ultima
3. Gabriel's preferred occupation
7. Where Marez boys were at the beginning of the novel
8. What the people were turned into
9. First grade teacher: Miss ___
12. Color of the god-carp
13. Died trying to warn Ultima of danger
15. Took Antonio to see the golden carp
17. What surrounded the town of Guadalupe
20. Author
23. Most forceful brother
24. Farming family
25. Coached in manners by her sister

Down
1. War-crazed murderer
2. Antonio expected to get answers from God after making it
3. Always running: ___ Kid
4. What owl took from Tenorio
5. Ultima's pet and spirit
6. Term of respect for Ultima: La ___
8. Ultima's occupation
10. What Antonio felt his first day at school
11. What a witch couldn't stand to wear
12. Town where Marez family lived
14. Wanted revenge for his brother's murder
16. Believed his house was cursed
18. His Indian told the story about the carp
19. Told Antonio the story of the carp
21. Home of Maria's farming relatives: El ___ De La Luna
22. Luna uncle who drove to warn Ultima

Bless Me Ultima Crossword 1 Answer Key

	1	2		3		4	5		6	
	L	U	C	A	S	V	A	Q	U	E	R	O		G	
		U		O		I			Y		7 W	A	R	
8 C	A	R	P	9 M	A	E	S	T	A	S	E	L	A	10 L
U				I		M			A				N	O
R		T		M		U	11 C		M		12 G	O	L	D	E	N
A				13 N	A	R	C	14 I	S	C	O	U		E	E
N				I			O		N		H		A		L
D	15 C	I	C	O	S				A			D	16 T	I
E				N		S				V		17 W	A	T	E	R	N
R	18 J		19 S						E		L		L		E
20 A	N	A	Y	A				21 P		Z		U		L		S
		S		M				U			22 P	P		E		S
		O		U				23 E	U	G	E	N	E		Z	
		N		E				R			D					
			24 L	U	N	A	25 T	H	E	R	E	S	A			
							O				O					

Across
1. Luna uncle cured by Ultima
3. Gabriel's preferred occupation
7. Where Marez boys were at the beginning of the novel
8. What the people were turned into
9. First grade teacher: Miss ___
12. Color of the god-carp
13. Died trying to warn Ultima of danger
15. Took Antonio to see the golden carp
17. What surrounded the town of Guadalupe
20. Author
23. Most forceful brother
24. Farming family
25. Coached in manners by her sister

Down
1. War-crazed murderer
2. Antonio expected to get answers from God after making it
3. Always running: ___ Kid
4. What owl took from Tenorio
5. Ultima's pet and spirit
6. Term of respect for Ultima: La ___
8. Ultima's occupation
10. What Antonio felt his first day at school
11. What a witch couldn't stand to wear
12. Town where Marez family lived
14. Wanted revenge for his brother's murder
16. Believed his house was cursed
18. His Indian told the story about the carp
19. Told Antonio the story of the carp
21. Home of Maria's farming relatives: El ___ De La Luna
22. Luna uncle who drove to warn Ultima

Blss Me Ultima Crossword 2

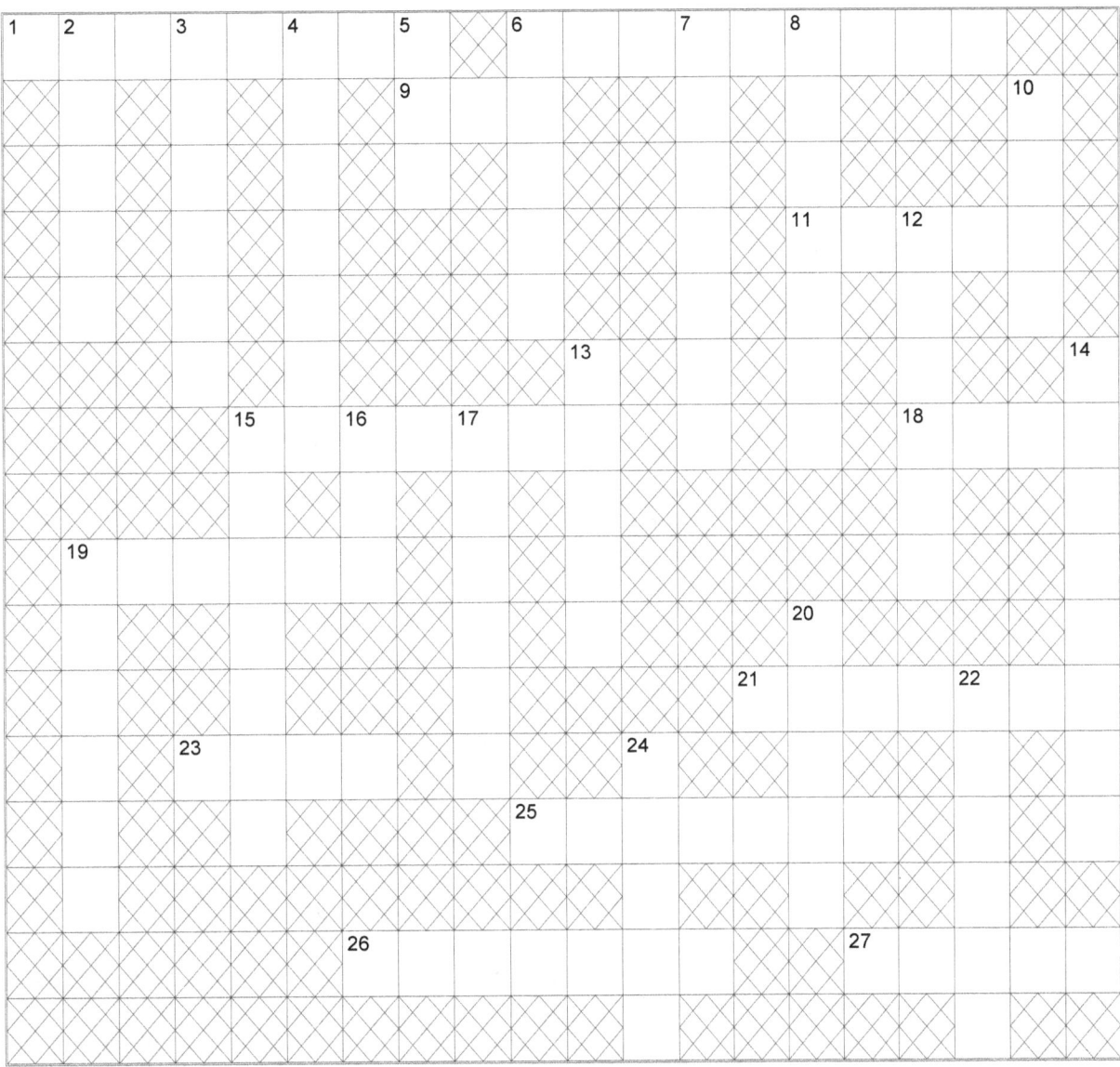

Across
1. Died trying to warn Ultima of danger
6. Ultima's occupation
9. Where Marez boys were at the beginning of the novel
11. What surrounded the town of Guadalupe
15. Coached in manners by her sister
18. Farming family
19. Term of respect for Ultima: La ___
21. Tree where Narcisco died
23. Took Antonio to see the golden carp
25. First grade teacher: Miss ___
26. Gabriel's preferred occupation
27. Ultima was accused of being one

Down
2. Author
3. Wanted revenge for his brother's murder
4. Antonio's native language
5. Ultima's pet and spirit
6. What a witch couldn't stand to wear
7. In conflict about his destiny
8. How Florence died
10. What the people were turned into
12. Believed his house was cursed
13. His Indian told the story about the carp
14. Ultima's home before coming to the Marez home: Las ___
15. Wanted revenge for his daughters' deaths
16. What owl took from Tenorio
17. Most forceful brother
19. Color of the god-carp
20. Luna uncle cured by Ultima
22. Home of Maria's farming relatives: El ___ De La Luna
24. Luna uncle who drove to warn Ultima

Bless Me Ultima Crossword 2 Answer Key

	1 N	2 A	3 R	4 C	5 I S C O		6 C	7 U	8 R	A	N	D	E	R	A	
		N		H		P	9 W	A	R		N		R			10 C
		A		A		P A L	L	O			T		O		11	12
		Y		V		N		S			O		11 W	A	12 T E R
		A		E		I		S			N		N		E	P
				Z		S			13 J	I		E	L		14 P
					15 T	16 H	17 E R E S A			18 L U N A
					E		Y	U		S			E			S
	19 G	R	A	N	D	E		G	O				Z			T
	O				O			E	N			20 L			U
	L				R			N			21 J	U	N	I	22 P E R
	D	23 C	I	C	O		E		24 P		C		U	A
	E				O	25 M	A	E	S	T	A	S		E	S
	N						D				S		R
				26 V	A	Q	U	E	R	O		27 W	I	T	C	H
								O					O

Across
1. Died trying to warn Ultima of danger
6. Ultima's occupation
9. Where Marez boys were at the beginning of the novel
11. What surrounded the town of Guadalupe
15. Coached in manners by her sister
18. Farming family
19. Term of respect for Ultima: La ___
21. Tree where Narciso died
23. Took Antonio to see the golden carp
25. First grade teacher: Miss ___
26. Gabriel's preferred occupation
27. Ultima was accused of being one

Down
2. Author
3. Wanted revenge for his brother's murder
4. Antonio's native language
5. Ultima's pet and spirit
6. What a witch couldn't stand to wear
7. In conflict about his destiny
8. How Florence died
10. What the people were turned into
12. Believed his house was cursed
13. His Indian told the story about the carp
14. Ultima's home before coming to the Marez home: Las ___
15. Wanted revenge for his daughters' deaths
16. What owl took from Tenorio
17. Most forceful brother
19. Color of the god-carp
20. Luna uncle cured by Ultima
22. Home of Maria's farming relatives: El ___ De La Luna
24. Luna uncle who drove to warn Ultima

Bless Me Ultima Crossword 3

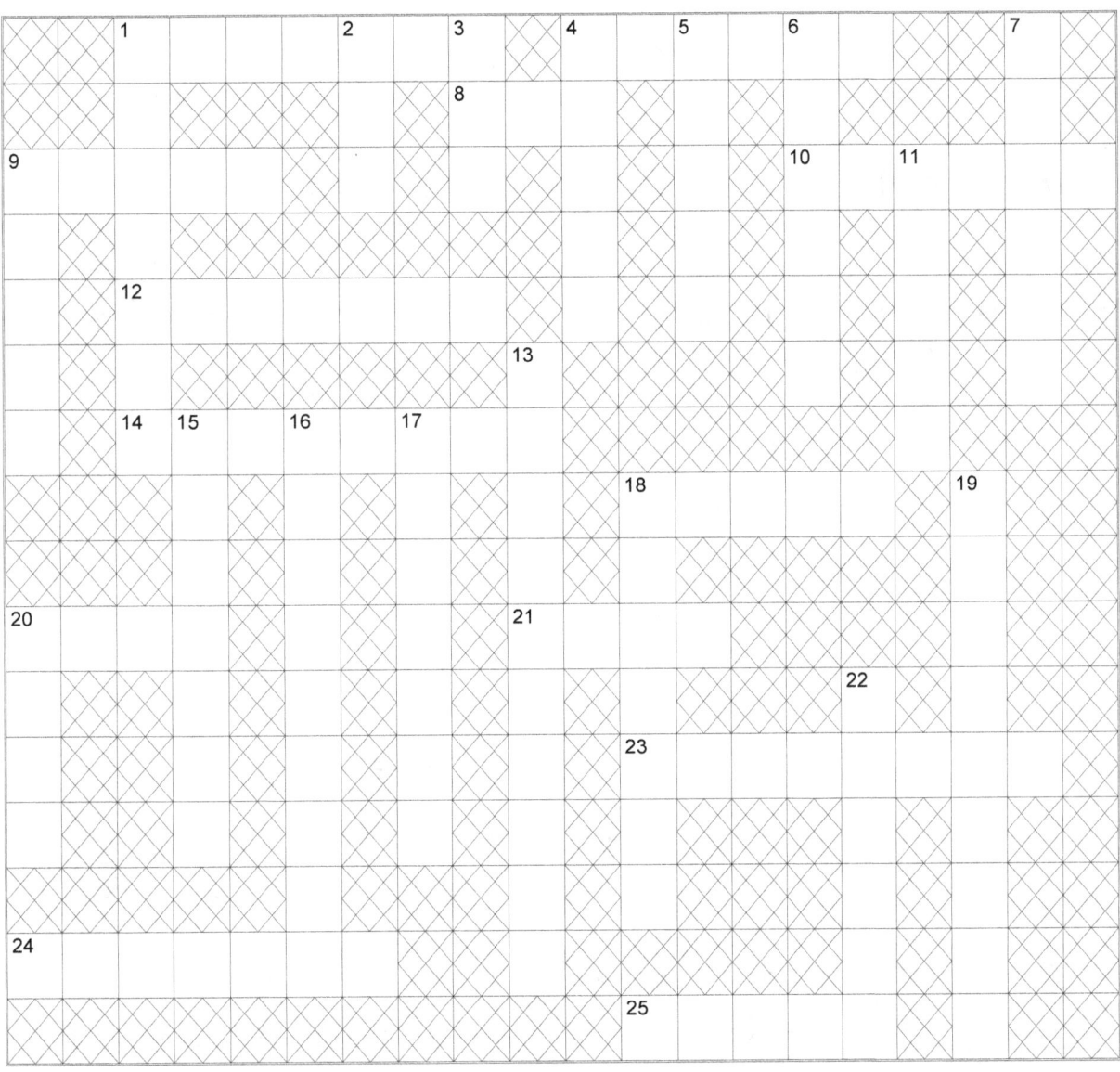

Across
1. Gabriel's preferred occupation
4. Wanted revenge for his brother's murder
8. Where Marez boys were at the beginning of the novel
9. What surrounded the town of Guadalupe
10. Color of the god-carp
12. First grade teacher: Miss ___
14. Died trying to warn Ultima of danger
18. His Indian told the story about the carp
20. Took Antonio to see the golden carp
21. Farming family
23. Ultima's home before coming to the Marez home: Las ___
24. Well-mannered Marez daughter
25. Luna uncle who drove to warn Ultima

Down
1. Always running: ___ Kid
2. What owl took from Tenorio
3. Ultima's pet and spirit
4. What a witch couldn't stand to wear
5. Author
6. Most forceful brother
7. Home of Maria's farming relatives: El ___ De La Luna
9. Ultima was accused of being one
11. Luna uncle cured by Ultima
13. What Antonio felt his first day at school
15. In conflict about his destiny
16. Ultima's occupation
17. Antonio's native language
18. Tree where Narcisco died
19. Town where Marez family lived
20. What the people were turned into
22. War-crazed murderer

Bless Me Ultima Crossword 3 Answer Key

		1 V	A	Q	2 U	E	R	3 O		4 C	5 H	A	6 V	E	Z		7 P
		I			Y			8 W	A	R		N		U			U
9 W	A	T	E	R		E	L			O		A		10 G	O	11 L	D	E	N
		I		A						S		Y		E		U			R
		12 M	A	E	S	T	A	S		S		A		N		C			T
		C		I				13 L						E		A			O
		H		14 N	15 A	R	16 C	I	17 S	C	O					S			
					N		U		P		N		18 J	A	S	O	N	19 G	
					T		R		A		E		U					U	
20 C	I	C	O		A		N		21 L	U	N	A						A	
A					N		N		I		I				22 L		D		
R					I		D		S		N		23 P	A	S	T	U	R	A	S
P					O		E		H		E		E		P		L	
							R				S		R		I		U	
24 D	E	B	O	R	A	H				S				T		P	
										25 P	E	D	R	O		E	

Across
1. Gabriel's preferred occupation
4. Wanted revenge for his brother's murder
8. Where Marez boys were at the beginning of the novel
9. What surrounded the town of Guadalupe
10. Color of the god-carp
12. First grade teacher: Miss ___
14. Died trying to warn Ultima of danger
18. His Indian told the story about the carp
20. Took Antonio to see the golden carp
21. Farming family
23. Ultima's home before coming to the Marez home: Las ___
24. Well-mannered Marez daughter
25. Luna uncle who drove to warn Ultima

Down
1. Always running: ___ Kid
2. What owl took from Tenorio
3. Ultima's pet and spirit
4. What a witch couldn't stand to wear
5. Author
6. Most forceful brother
7. Home of Maria's farming relatives: El ___ De La Luna
9. Ultima was accused of being one
11. Luna uncle cured by Ultima
13. What Antonio felt his first day at school
15. In conflict about his destiny
16. Ultima's occupation
17. Antonio's native language
18. Tree where Narcisco died
19. Town where Marez family lived
20. What the people were turned into
22. War-crazed murderer

Bless Me Ultima Crossword 4

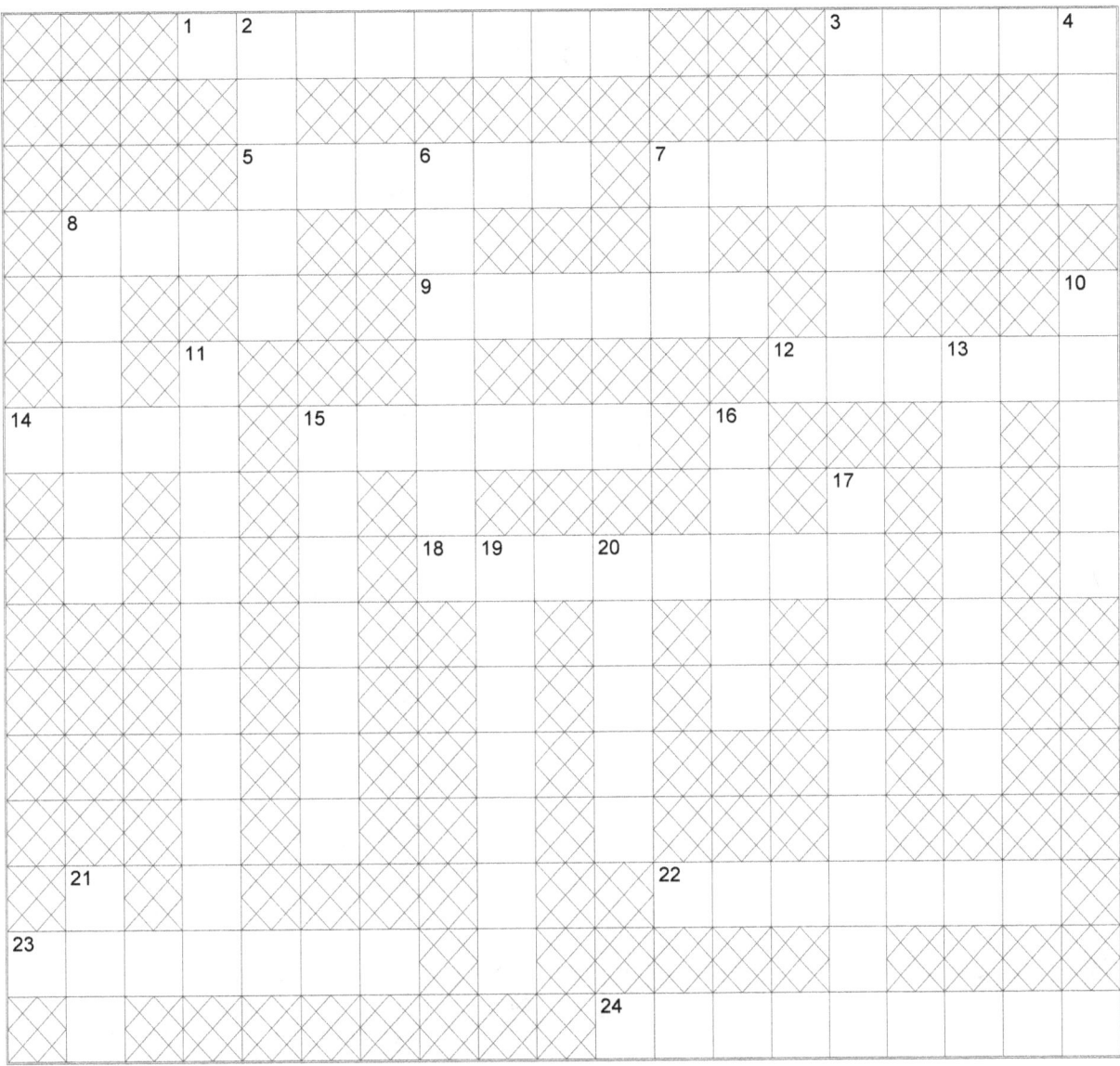

Across
1. Believed he had never sinned
3. Luna uncle who drove to warn Ultima
5. Wanted revenge for his brother's murder
7. Most forceful brother
8. Farming family
9. Believed his house was cursed
12. Color of the god-carp
14. Took Antonio to see the golden carp
15. Told Antonio the story of the carp
18. Died trying to warn Ultima of danger
22. Tree where Narcisco died
23. First grade teacher: Miss ___
24. Ultima's occupation

Down
2. Luna uncle cured by Ultima
3. Home of Maria's farming relatives: El ___ De La Luna
4. Ultima's pet and spirit
6. Always running: ___ Kid
7. What owl took from Tenorio
8. War-crazed murderer
10. Author
11. What Antonio felt his first day at school
13. How Florence died
15. Antonio's native language
16. His Indian told the story about the carp
17. Antonio expected to get answers from God after making it
19. In conflict about his destiny
20. What a witch couldn't stand to wear
21. Where Marez boys were at the beginning of the novel

Bless Me Ultima Crossword 4 Answer Key

		1 F	2 L	O	R	E	N	C	E			3 P	E	D	R	4 O
			U									U				W
			5 C	H	A	6 V	E	Z		7 E	U	G	E	N	E	L
	8 L	U	N	A		I				Y		R				
	U		S			9 T	E	L	L	E	Z		T			10 A
	P		11 L			A					12 G	O	L	13 D	E	N
14 C	I	C	O		15 S	A	M	U	E	L	16 J			R		A
	T		N		P		I				A	17 C		O		Y
	O		E		A	18 N	19 A	R	20 C	I	S	C	O	W		A
			L		N		N		R		O		M	N		
			I		I		T		O		N		M	E		
			N		S		O		S				U	D		
			E		H		N		S				N			
	21 W		S				I			22 J	U	N	I	P	E	R
23 M	A	E	S	T	A	S	O						O			
	R								24 C	U	R	A	N	D	E	R	A

Across
1. Believed he had never sinned
3. Luna uncle who drove to warn Ultima
5. Wanted revenge for his brother's murder
7. Most forceful brother
8. Farming family
9. Believed his house was cursed
12. Color of the god-carp
14. Took Antonio to see the golden carp
15. Told Antonio the story of the carp
18. Died trying to warn Ultima of danger
22. Tree where Narciso died
23. First grade teacher: Miss ___
24. Ultima's occupation

Down
2. Luna uncle cured by Ultima
3. Home of Maria's farming relatives: El ___ De La Luna
4. Ultima's pet and spirit
6. Always running: ___ Kid
7. What owl took from Tenorio
8. War-crazed murderer
10. Author
11. What Antonio felt his first day at school
13. How Florence died
15. Antonio's native language
16. His Indian told the story about the carp
17. Antonio expected to get answers from God after making it
19. In conflict about his destiny
20. What a witch couldn't stand to wear
21. Where Marez boys were at the beginning of the novel

BLESS ME UNIT

CHAVEZ	GUADALUPE	WATER	VAQUERO	CICO
THERESA	TENORIO	MAESTAS	EYE	TELLEZ
WAR	CARP	FREE SPACE	DROWNED	CURANDERA
JUNIPER	PASTURAS	OWL	ANTONIO	NARCISCO
JASON	EUGENE	PEDRO	CROSS	GOLDEN

BLESS ME UNIT

GRANDE	PUERTO	LONELINESS	SAMUEL	COMMUNION
LUNA	LUPITO	SPANISH	DEBORAH	LUCAS
FLORENCE	ANAYA	FREE SPACE	WITCH	GOLDEN
CROSS	PEDRO	EUGENE	JASON	NARCISCO
ANTONIO	OWL	PASTURAS	JUNIPER	CURANDERA

BLESS ME UNIT

DEBORAH	ANAYA	GOLDEN	OWL	CHAVEZ
LONELINESS	ANTONIO	LUPITO	SAMUEL	PUERTO
EUGENE	CURANDERA	FREE SPACE	VITAMIN	CARP
FLORENCE	DROWNED	TREMENTINA	SPANISH	GRANDE
TELLEZ	WATER	WAR	JUNIPER	THERESA

BLESS ME UNIT

JASON	LUCAS	LUNA	PASTURAS	CROSS
VAQUERO	CICO	EYE	MAESTAS	WITCH
TENORIO	NARCISCO	FREE SPACE	GUADALUPE	THERESA
JUNIPER	WAR	WATER	TELLEZ	GRANDE
SPANISH	TREMENTINA	DROWNED	FLORENCE	CARP

BLESS ME UNIT

JUNIPER	TREMENTINA	LUCAS	SAMUEL	TELLEZ
COMMUNION	VAQUERO	LUPITO	ANAYA	CICO
CHAVEZ	EUGENE	FREE SPACE	DEBORAH	EYE
CARP	WITCH	GOLDEN	WAR	PUERTO
LONELINESS	OWL	TENORIO	SPANISH	CROSS

BLESS ME UNIT

ANTONIO	THERESA	PASTURAS	LUNA	NARCISCO
PEDRO	GRANDE	JASON	FLORENCE	VITAMIN
MAESTAS	GUADALUPE	FREE SPACE	WATER	CROSS
SPANISH	TENORIO	OWL	LONELINESS	PUERTO
WAR	GOLDEN	WITCH	CARP	EYE

BLESS ME UNIT

PUERTO	LUNA	LUCAS	DROWNED	DEBORAH
LONELINESS	THERESA	PASTURAS	VITAMIN	VAQUERO
CARP	EUGENE	FREE SPACE	TELLEZ	FLORENCE
TREMENTINA	JASON	EYE	ANTONIO	CICO
JUNIPER	LUPITO	GUADALUPE	CHAVEZ	MAESTAS

BLESS ME UNIT

ANAYA	GRANDE	SPANISH	PEDRO	SAMUEL
WAR	WATER	GOLDEN	OWL	NARCISCO
TENORIO	CURANDERA	FREE SPACE	COMMUNION	MAESTAS
CHAVEZ	GUADALUPE	LUPITO	JUNIPER	CICO
ANTONIO	EYE	JASON	TREMENTINA	FLORENCE

BLESS ME UNIT

GUADALUPE	TREMENTINA	PEDRO	VAQUERO	TELLEZ
WATER	TENORIO	DROWNED	CROSS	CHAVEZ
SPANISH	FLORENCE	FREE SPACE	JASON	ANAYA
PUERTO	VITAMIN	LUNA	DEBORAH	CICO
EUGENE	ANTONIO	PASTURAS	JUNIPER	CURANDERA

BLESS ME UNIT

GOLDEN	SAMUEL	LUPITO	OWL	CARP
NARCISCO	GRANDE	LUCAS	THERESA	EYE
WITCH	LONELINESS	FREE SPACE	MAESTAS	CURANDERA
JUNIPER	PASTURAS	ANTONIO	EUGENE	CICO
DEBORAH	LUNA	VITAMIN	PUERTO	ANAYA

BLESS ME UNIT

COMMUNION	OWL	LUPITO	SPANISH	ANAYA
DEBORAH	CURANDERA	ANTONIO	JUNIPER	LONELINESS
PEDRO	TREMENTINA	FREE SPACE	CARP	DROWNED
FLORENCE	WITCH	EUGENE	CROSS	THERESA
GOLDEN	NARCISCO	CICO	VAQUERO	TELLEZ

BLESS ME UNIT

JASON	CHAVEZ	SAMUEL	LUCAS	TENORIO
PUERTO	GUADALUPE	MAESTAS	VITAMIN	GRANDE
LUNA	PASTURAS	FREE SPACE	EYE	TELLEZ
VAQUERO	CICO	NARCISCO	GOLDEN	THERESA
CROSS	EUGENE	WITCH	FLORENCE	DROWNED

BLESS ME UNIT

LUNA	FLORENCE	CHAVEZ	DROWNED	COMMUNION
WITCH	VITAMIN	GRANDE	PEDRO	LUPITO
ANTONIO	NARCISCO	FREE SPACE	THERESA	VAQUERO
GOLDEN	CROSS	LUCAS	PASTURAS	TELLEZ
SPANISH	WAR	OWL	TREMENTINA	EYE

BLESS ME UNIT

CICO	EUGENE	JUNIPER	PUERTO	TENORIO
CARP	SAMUEL	MAESTAS	ANAYA	DEBORAH
GUADALUPE	LONELINESS	FREE SPACE	WATER	EYE
TREMENTINA	OWL	WAR	SPANISH	TELLEZ
PASTURAS	LUCAS	CROSS	GOLDEN	VAQUERO

BLESS ME UNIT

VITAMIN	MAESTAS	GRANDE	CROSS	TREMENTINA
TELLEZ	SAMUEL	PUERTO	VAQUERO	CICO
GOLDEN	THERESA	FREE SPACE	CHAVEZ	PEDRO
PASTURAS	WITCH	CURANDERA	WAR	LUPITO
NARCISCO	LONELINESS	ANAYA	EYE	LUNA

BLESS ME UNIT

DEBORAH	SPANISH	LUCAS	JASON	EUGENE
ANTONIO	GUADALUPE	WATER	JUNIPER	OWL
DROWNED	CARP	FREE SPACE	COMMUNION	LUNA
EYE	ANAYA	LONELINESS	NARCISCO	LUPITO
WAR	CURANDERA	WITCH	PASTURAS	PEDRO

BLESS ME UNIT

CARP	SPANISH	ANTONIO	EUGENE	PASTURAS
LUNA	MAESTAS	CICO	JASON	THERESA
PUERTO	LUCAS	FREE SPACE	GUADALUPE	DEBORAH
EYE	WAR	PEDRO	DROWNED	WATER
TENORIO	TELLEZ	VITAMIN	NARCISCO	CROSS

BLESS ME UNIT

WITCH	GRANDE	ANAYA	CURANDERA	SAMUEL
LUPITO	VAQUERO	FLORENCE	LONELINESS	JUNIPER
COMMUNION	CHAVEZ	FREE SPACE	TREMENTINA	CROSS
NARCISCO	VITAMIN	TELLEZ	TENORIO	WATER
DROWNED	PEDRO	WAR	EYE	DEBORAH

BLESS ME UNIT

WITCH	VITAMIN	CHAVEZ	DEBORAH	CROSS
PUERTO	TELLEZ	LUPITO	DROWNED	SPANISH
SAMUEL	GUADALUPE	FREE SPACE	JUNIPER	WATER
CICO	ANAYA	LUNA	MAESTAS	PASTURAS
CARP	EYE	ANTONIO	LUCAS	COMMUNION

BLESS ME UNIT

OWL	GRANDE	CURANDERA	LONELINESS	THERESA
GOLDEN	JASON	EUGENE	WAR	NARCISCO
VAQUERO	TREMENTINA	FREE SPACE	TENORIO	COMMUNION
LUCAS	ANTONIO	EYE	CARP	PASTURAS
MAESTAS	LUNA	ANAYA	CICO	WATER

BLESS ME UNIT

WATER	NARCISO	WAR	DROWNED	SPANISH
OWL	CICO	DEBORAH	GUADALUPE	CURANDERA
CARP	PUERTO	FREE SPACE	PEDRO	PASTURAS
JUNIPER	EUGENE	TREMENTINA	GRANDE	LONELINESS
FLORENCE	ANAYA	LUCAS	LUPITO	GOLDEN

BLESS ME UNIT

VAQUERO	WITCH	CHAVEZ	JASON	COMMUNION
SAMUEL	THERESA	LUNA	EYE	TENORIO
ANTONIO	CROSS	FREE SPACE	TELLEZ	GOLDEN
LUPITO	LUCAS	ANAYA	FLORENCE	LONELINESS
GRANDE	TREMENTINA	EUGENE	JUNIPER	PASTURAS

BLESS ME UNIT

TREMENTINA	SAMUEL	VITAMIN	GRANDE	DROWNED
LUNA	TELLEZ	TENORIO	OWL	CHAVEZ
FLORENCE	GUADALUPE	FREE SPACE	EYE	CICO
CURANDERA	ANTONIO	GOLDEN	PUERTO	JUNIPER
CARP	LUPITO	EUGENE	WAR	SPANISH

BLESS ME UNIT

WITCH	PASTURAS	CROSS	THERESA	DEBORAH
WATER	COMMUNION	MAESTAS	LONELINESS	JASON
ANAYA	VAQUERO	FREE SPACE	PEDRO	SPANISH
WAR	EUGENE	LUPITO	CARP	JUNIPER
PUERTO	GOLDEN	ANTONIO	CURANDERA	CICO

BLESS ME UNIT

LUNA	GUADALUPE	SPANISH	TREMENTINA	ANTONIO
MAESTAS	WATER	PEDRO	DEBORAH	FLORENCE
PUERTO	TENORIO	FREE SPACE	TELLEZ	WITCH
GOLDEN	WAR	CARP	JUNIPER	JASON
SAMUEL	OWL	CHAVEZ	COMMUNION	GRANDE

BLESS ME UNIT

EUGENE	ANAYA	LUPITO	VITAMIN	VAQUERO
DROWNED	PASTURAS	LUCAS	CROSS	THERESA
EYE	NARCISCO	FREE SPACE	CICO	GRANDE
COMMUNION	CHAVEZ	OWL	SAMUEL	JASON
JUNIPER	CARP	WAR	GOLDEN	WITCH

BLESS ME UNIT

LUNA	MAESTAS	TELLEZ	PASTURAS	VITAMIN
CICO	CROSS	CARP	PUERTO	EUGENE
PEDRO	EYE	FREE SPACE	TREMENTINA	FLORENCE
JASON	COMMUNION	GRANDE	SPANISH	WITCH
CHAVEZ	LONELINESS	ANAYA	THERESA	LUCAS

BLESS ME UNIT

SAMUEL	NARCISCO	DEBORAH	CURANDERA	WAR
OWL	DROWNED	TENORIO	GOLDEN	ANTONIO
GUADALUPE	VAQUERO	FREE SPACE	LUPITO	LUCAS
THERESA	ANAYA	LONELINESS	CHAVEZ	WITCH
SPANISH	GRANDE	COMMUNION	JASON	FLORENCE

BLESS ME UNIT

VITAMIN	CHAVEZ	LUNA	EYE	DEBORAH
CURANDERA	TELLEZ	COMMUNION	GUADALUPE	CARP
DROWNED	EUGENE	FREE SPACE	CROSS	PEDRO
MAESTAS	LUCAS	ANAYA	SPANISH	OWL
TENORIO	NARCISCO	ANTONIO	THERESA	WITCH

BLESS ME UNIT

PASTURAS	JUNIPER	WATER	GOLDEN	SAMUEL
LONELINESS	CICO	TREMENTINA	GRANDE	VAQUERO
JASON	LUPITO	FREE SPACE	PUERTO	WITCH
THERESA	ANTONIO	NARCISCO	TENORIO	OWL
SPANISH	ANAYA	LUCAS	MAESTAS	PEDRO

Copyrighted

BLESS ME UNIT

EYE	THERESA	FLORENCE	NARCISCO	CARP
LUCAS	TENORIO	DROWNED	SAMUEL	SPANISH
WATER	CROSS	FREE SPACE	EUGENE	VITAMIN
OWL	COMMUNION	GOLDEN	VAQUERO	GUADALUPE
MAESTAS	WITCH	LUNA	PEDRO	ANAYA

BLESS ME UNIT

JUNIPER	TELLEZ	CHAVEZ	LONELINESS	GRANDE
WAR	PASTURAS	DEBORAH	JASON	CURANDERA
CICO	LUPITO	FREE SPACE	ANTONIO	ANAYA
PEDRO	LUNA	WITCH	MAESTAS	GUADALUPE
VAQUERO	GOLDEN	COMMUNION	OWL	VITAMIN

Bless Me Ultima Vocabulary Word List

No.	Word	Clue/Definition
1.	ABRUPTLY	Suddenly
2.	ACRID	Unpleasantly sharp, pungent, or bitter to smell
3.	ADMONISHED	Reproved gently but earnestly
4.	ARROGANT	Making claims to unwarranted importance
5.	AUDACITY	Fearlessness; boldness
6.	BLEMISH	Imperfection that mars or impairs
7.	BRISTLED	Caused to stand erect; stiffened
8.	CARAVAN	Company of travelers journeying together
9.	CLAMORED	Made a loud, sustained noise or outcry
10.	COMMOTION	Agitated disturbance
11.	CONTEMPTUOUSLY	Disdainfully; scornfully
12.	COUNTERED	Offered in response
13.	CROONED	Sung softly or in a humming way
14.	DEBRIS	Rubble or wreckage
15.	DEFIANCE	Bold resistance
16.	DESECRATED	Violated the sacredness of; profaned
17.	DISQUIETUDE	Worried unease; anxiety
18.	DIVULGED	Made known something private or secret
19.	DRONE	Continuous, low, dull humming sound
20.	DYSENTERY	Inflammatory disorder of the lower intestinal tract
21.	ELATION	Pride; joy
22.	EMACIATED	Made extremely thin, especially as a result of starvation
23.	EMANATED	Came forth or sent forth, as from a source
24.	EMPHATICALLY	Positively; definitely
25.	ENDOWED	Provided with property or income
26.	ENDURES	Continues in existence; lasts
27.	ETCHED	Cut into the surface of
28.	EXASPERATION	Anger or impatience
29.	EXORCISE	Free from evil spirits or malign influences
30.	EXUBERANT	Joyous; full of high spirits
31.	FLEETING	Moving swiftly; rapid or nimble
32.	FORAGE	Wander in search of food or provisions
33.	FORSAKING	Giving up something formerly held dear
34.	FURROW	A rut, groove, or narrow depression
35.	HERESY	Dissension from dogma by a professed believer
36.	ILLUMINATED	Lit up
37.	IMPENDING	About to take place
38.	INCANTATION	Ritual recitation of charms or spells to produce magic
39.	INDEBTED	Morally, socially, or legally obliged to another; beholden
40.	INSTINCTIVELY	Done by innate aptitude
41.	INTERMINABLE	Endless
42.	INTRUSION	Rude or inappropriate entrance
43.	IRREVOCABLE	Impossible to retract or take back
44.	LURKING	Lying in wait, as in ambush
45.	MANIPULATED	Influenced or managed shrewdly or deviously
46.	MELEE	Violent free-for-all
47.	MOTES	Very small particles; specks
48.	OBSTACLES	Things that oppose or stand in the way of
49.	PERDITION	Loss of soul; eternal damnation
50.	PHANTOMS	Ghosts or apparitions
51.	PULSATING	Expanding and contracting rhythmically; beating

Bless Me Ultima Vocabulary Word List Continued

No.	Word	Clue/Definition
52.	QUAVERED	Trembled
53.	RESIGNED	Unresistingly accepting
54.	RESOLUTION	Firm determination
55.	REVERBERATING	Resounding in a series of echoes
56.	SARDONICALLY	Scornfully or cynically mocking
57.	SCOFFED	Mocked or treated with derision
58.	SHEATHS	Cases for sword or knife blades
59.	STOICALLY	Unaffected by pleasure or pain; impassively
60.	STUPOR	State of mental numbness; a daze
61.	SUBSIDED	Became less agitated or active
62.	SUCCULENT	Full of juice or sap; juicy
63.	TENACIOUSLY	Persistently
64.	TORMENTED	Caused great pain or anguish
65.	TRANSFIXED	Rendered motionless, as with terror or amazement
66.	UNPERTURBED	Not disturbed or confused
67.	VAGABONDS	People without permanent homes
68.	VIGILANTES	Those who take law enforcement upon themselves
69.	WROUGHT	Created; put together

Bless Me Ultima Vocabulary Fill In The Blank 1

_____ 1. Made a loud, sustained noise or outcry

_____ 2. Came forth or sent forth, as from a source

_____ 3. Made known something private or secret

_____ 4. Violated the sacredness of; profaned

_____ 5. Free from evil spirits or malign influences

_____ 6. Anger or impatience

_____ 7. Mocked or treated with derision

_____ 8. Moving swiftly; rapid or nimble

_____ 9. Expanding and contracting rhythmically; beating

_____ 10. Offered in response

_____ 11. Rude or inappropriate entrance

_____ 12. About to take place

_____ 13. Lit up

_____ 14. Sung softly or in a humming way

_____ 15. Done by innate aptitude

_____ 16. Positively; definitely

_____ 17. Cut into the surface of

_____ 18. Not disturbed or confused

_____ 19. Rubble or wreckage

_____ 20. Loss of soul; eternal damnation

Bless Me Ultima Vocabulary Fill In The Blank 1 Answer Key

CLAMORED	1. Made a loud, sustained noise or outcry
EMANATED	2. Came forth or sent forth, as from a source
DIVULGED	3. Made known something private or secret
DESECRATED	4. Violated the sacredness of; profaned
EXORCISE	5. Free from evil spirits or malign influences
EXASPERATION	6. Anger or impatience
SCOFFED	7. Mocked or treated with derision
FLEETING	8. Moving swiftly; rapid or nimble
PULSATING	9. Expanding and contracting rhythmically; beating
COUNTERED	10. Offered in response
INTRUSION	11. Rude or inappropriate entrance
IMPENDING	12. About to take place
ILLUMINATED	13. Lit up
CROONED	14. Sung softly or in a humming way
INSTINCTIVELY	15. Done by innate aptitude
EMPHATICALLY	16. Positively; definitely
ETCHED	17. Cut into the surface of
UNPERTURBED	18. Not disturbed or confused
DEBRIS	19. Rubble or wreckage
PERDITION	20. Loss of soul; eternal damnation

Bless Me Ultima Vocabulary Fill In The Blank 2

1. Making claims to unwarranted importance
2. Rubble or wreckage
3. Influenced or managed shrewdly or deviously
4. Reproved gently but earnestly
5. Continuous, low, dull humming sound
6. Impossible to retract or take back
7. Bold resistance
8. Mocked or treated with derision
9. People without permanent homes
10. Unpleasantly sharp, pungent, or bitter to smell
11. Anger or impatience
12. Cut into the surface of
13. Persistently
14. Agitated disturbance
15. Offered in response
16. Those who take law enforcement upon themselves
17. Moving swiftly; rapid or nimble
18. Pride; joy
19. A rut, groove, or narrow depression
20. Unaffected by pleasure or pain; impassively

Bless Me Ultima Vocabulary Fill In The Blank 2 Answer Key

ARROGANT	1. Making claims to unwarranted importance
DEBRIS	2. Rubble or wreckage
MANIPULATED	3. Influenced or managed shrewdly or deviously
ADMONISHED	4. Reproved gently but earnestly
DRONE	5. Continuous, low, dull humming sound
IRREVOCABLE	6. Impossible to retract or take back
DEFIANCE	7. Bold resistance
SCOFFED	8. Mocked or treated with derision
VAGABONDS	9. People without permanent homes
ACRID	10. Unpleasantly sharp, pungent, or bitter to smell
EXASPERATION	11. Anger or impatience
ETCHED	12. Cut into the surface of
TENACIOUSLY	13. Persistently
COMMOTION	14. Agitated disturbance
COUNTERED	15. Offered in response
VIGILANTES	16. Those who take law enforcement upon themselves
FLEETING	17. Moving swiftly; rapid or nimble
ELATION	18. Pride; joy
FURROW	19. A rut, groove, or narrow depression
STOICALLY	20. Unaffected by pleasure or pain; impassively

Bless Me Ultima Vocabulary Fill In The Blank 3

_____ 1. Persistently

_____ 2. Rubble or wreckage

_____ 3. People without permanent homes

_____ 4. Giving up something formerly held dear

_____ 5. Became less agitated or active

_____ 6. Making claims to unwarranted importance

_____ 7. Ritual recitation of charms or spells to produce magic

_____ 8. State of mental numbness; a daze

_____ 9. Pride; joy

_____ 10. Resounding in a series of echoes

_____ 11. Worried unease; anxiety

_____ 12. Expanding and contracting rhythmically; beating

_____ 13. Violated the sacredness of; profaned

_____ 14. Trembled

_____ 15. Lit up

_____ 16. Violent free-for-all

_____ 17. Made extremely thin, especially as a result of starvation

_____ 18. Fearlessness; boldness

_____ 19. Joyous; full of high spirits

_____ 20. Lying in wait, as in ambush

Bless Me Ultima Vocabulary Fill In The Blank 3 Answer Key

TENACIOUSLY	1. Persistently
DEBRIS	2. Rubble or wreckage
VAGABONDS	3. People without permanent homes
FORSAKING	4. Giving up something formerly held dear
SUBSIDED	5. Became less agitated or active
ARROGANT	6. Making claims to unwarranted importance
INCANTATION	7. Ritual recitation of charms or spells to produce magic
STUPOR	8. State of mental numbness; a daze
ELATION	9. Pride; joy
REVERBERATING	10. Resounding in a series of echoes
DISQUIETUDE	11. Worried unease; anxiety
PULSATING	12. Expanding and contracting rhythmically; beating
DESECRATED	13. Violated the sacredness of; profaned
QUAVERED	14. Trembled
ILLUMINATED	15. Lit up
MELEE	16. Violent free-for-all
EMACIATED	17. Made extremely thin, especially as a result of starvation
AUDACITY	18. Fearlessness; boldness
EXUBERANT	19. Joyous; full of high spirits
LURKING	20. Lying in wait, as in ambush

Bless Me Ultima Vocabulary Fill In The Blank 4

1. Rude or inappropriate entrance
2. Endless
3. Anger or impatience
4. Continues in existence; lasts
5. Scornfully or cynically mocking
6. Loss of soul; eternal damnation
7. Cut into the surface of
8. Not disturbed or confused
9. Agitated disturbance
10. Disdainfully; scornfully
11. Continuous, low, dull humming sound
12. Reproved gently but earnestly
13. Worried unease; anxiety
14. Trembled
15. Provided with property or income
16. Resounding in a series of echoes
17. Ghosts or apparitions
18. Violated the sacredness of; profaned
19. Things that oppose or stand in the way of
20. Caused great pain or anguish

Bless Me Ultima Vocabulary Fill In The Blank 4 Answer Key

INTRUSION	1.	Rude or inappropriate entrance
INTERMINABLE	2.	Endless
EXASPERATION	3.	Anger or impatience
ENDURES	4.	Continues in existence; lasts
SARDONICALLY	5.	Scornfully or cynically mocking
PERDITION	6.	Loss of soul; eternal damnation
ETCHED	7.	Cut into the surface of
UNPERTURBED	8.	Not disturbed or confused
COMMOTION	9.	Agitated disturbance
CONTEMPTUOUSLY	10.	Disdainfully; scornfully
DRONE	11.	Continuous, low, dull humming sound
ADMONISHED	12.	Reproved gently but earnestly
DISQUIETUDE	13.	Worried unease; anxiety
QUAVERED	14.	Trembled
ENDOWED	15.	Provided with property or income
REVERBERATING	16.	Resounding in a series of echoes
PHANTOMS	17.	Ghosts or apparitions
DESECRATED	18.	Violated the sacredness of; profaned
OBSTACLES	19.	Things that oppose or stand in the way of
TORMENTED	20.	Caused great pain or anguish

Bless Me Ultima Vocabulary Matching 1

___ 1. SCOFFED   A. Free from evil spirits or malign influences
___ 2. SARDONICALLY   B. Very small particles; specks
___ 3. VIGILANTES   C. Ghosts or apparitions
___ 4. UNPERTURBED   D. Inflammatory disorder of the lower intestinal tract
___ 5. TENACIOUSLY   E. Loss of soul; eternal damnation
___ 6. COUNTERED   F. Endless
___ 7. PULSATING   G. Offered in response
___ 8. EXORCISE   H. Trembled
___ 9. TORMENTED   I. Persistently
___10. EXUBERANT   J. Provided with property or income
___11. INTERMINABLE   K. Company of travelers journeying together
___12. CARAVAN   L. Anger or impatience
___13. DIVULGED   M. Influenced or managed shrewdly or deviously
___14. SHEATHS   N. Made known something private or secret
___15. QUAVERED   O. Cases for sword or knife blades
___16. MANIPULATED   P. Caused great pain or anguish
___17. PHANTOMS   Q. Scornfully or cynically mocking
___18. PERDITION   R. State of mental numbness; a daze
___19. ADMONISHED   S. Reproved gently but earnestly
___20. ENDOWED   T. Joyous; full of high spirits
___21. MOTES   U. Expanding and contracting rhythmically; beating
___22. STUPOR   V. Those who take law enforcement upon themselves
___23. DYSENTERY   W. Created; put together
___24. EXASPERATION   X. Mocked or treated with derision
___25. WROUGHT   Y. Not disturbed or confused

Bless Me Ultima Vocabulary Matching 1 Answer Key

X - 1. SCOFFED	A.	Free from evil spirits or malign influences
Q - 2. SARDONICALLY	B.	Very small particles; specks
V - 3. VIGILANTES	C.	Ghosts or apparitions
Y - 4. UNPERTURBED	D.	Inflammatory disorder of the lower intestinal tract
I - 5. TENACIOUSLY	E.	Loss of soul; eternal damnation
G - 6. COUNTERED	F.	Endless
U - 7. PULSATING	G.	Offered in response
A - 8. EXORCISE	H.	Trembled
P - 9. TORMENTED	I.	Persistently
T - 10. EXUBERANT	J.	Provided with property or income
F - 11. INTERMINABLE	K.	Company of travelers journeying together
K - 12. CARAVAN	L.	Anger or impatience
N - 13. DIVULGED	M.	Influenced or managed shrewdly or deviously
O - 14. SHEATHS	N.	Made known something private or secret
H - 15. QUAVERED	O.	Cases for sword or knife blades
M - 16. MANIPULATED	P.	Caused great pain or anguish
C - 17. PHANTOMS	Q.	Scornfully or cynically mocking
E - 18. PERDITION	R.	State of mental numbness; a daze
S - 19. ADMONISHED	S.	Reproved gently but earnestly
J - 20. ENDOWED	T.	Joyous; full of high spirits
B - 21. MOTES	U.	Expanding and contracting rhythmically; beating
R - 22. STUPOR	V.	Those who take law enforcement upon themselves
D - 23. DYSENTERY	W.	Created; put together
L - 24. EXASPERATION	X.	Mocked or treated with derision
W - 25. WROUGHT	Y.	Not disturbed or confused

Bless Me Ultima Vocabulary Matching 2

___ 1. ELATION A. Wander in search of food or provisions
___ 2. UNPERTURBED B. Lying in wait, as in ambush
___ 3. ENDURES C. Pride; joy
___ 4. INTRUSION D. Rendered motionless, as with terror or amazement
___ 5. FORSAKING E. Very small particles; specks
___ 6. TENACIOUSLY F. Not disturbed or confused
___ 7. VIGILANTES G. Persistently
___ 8. ABRUPTLY H. Morally, socially, or legally obliged to another; beholden
___ 9. DISQUIETUDE I. Created; put together
___10. ENDOWED J. Giving up something formerly held dear
___11. DIVULGED K. Worried unease; anxiety
___12. CONTEMPTUOUSLY L. Continues in existence; lasts
___13. FORAGE M. Bold resistance
___14. PULSATING N. Suddenly
___15. MOTES O. Those who take law enforcement upon themselves
___16. TRANSFIXED P. Trembled
___17. EMANATED Q. Disdainfully; scornfully
___18. INDEBTED R. Provided with property or income
___19. QUAVERED S. Expanding and contracting rhythmically; beating
___20. LURKING T. Came forth or sent forth, as from a source
___21. ARROGANT U. Making claims to unwarranted importance
___22. DEFIANCE V. Rude or inappropriate entrance
___23. WROUGHT W. Made known something private or secret
___24. EXASPERATION X. Done by innate aptitude
___25. INSTINCTIVELY Y. Anger or impatience

Bless Me Ultima Vocabulary Matching 2 Answer Key

C - 1. ELATION
F - 2. UNPERTURBED
L - 3. ENDURES
V - 4. INTRUSION
J - 5. FORSAKING
G - 6. TENACIOUSLY
O - 7. VIGILANTES
N - 8. ABRUPTLY
K - 9. DISQUIETUDE
R - 10. ENDOWED
W - 11. DIVULGED
Q - 12. CONTEMPTUOUSLY
A - 13. FORAGE
S - 14. PULSATING
E - 15. MOTES
D - 16. TRANSFIXED
T - 17. EMANATED
H - 18. INDEBTED
P - 19. QUAVERED
B - 20. LURKING
U - 21. ARROGANT
M - 22. DEFIANCE
I - 23. WROUGHT
Y - 24. EXASPERATION
X - 25. INSTINCTIVELY

A. Wander in search of food or provisions
B. Lying in wait, as in ambush
C. Pride; joy
D. Rendered motionless, as with terror or amazement
E. Very small particles; specks
F. Not disturbed or confused
G. Persistently
H. Morally, socially, or legally obliged to another; beholden
I. Created; put together
J. Giving up something formerly held dear
K. Worried unease; anxiety
L. Continues in existence; lasts
M. Bold resistance
N. Suddenly
O. Those who take law enforcement upon themselves
P. Trembled
Q. Disdainfully; scornfully
R. Provided with property or income
S. Expanding and contracting rhythmically; beating
T. Came forth or sent forth, as from a source
U. Making claims to unwarranted importance
V. Rude or inappropriate entrance
W. Made known something private or secret
X. Done by innate aptitude
Y. Anger or impatience

Bless Me Ultima Vocabulary Matching 3

___ 1. FORSAKING   A. About to take place
___ 2. PHANTOMS   B. Making claims to unwarranted importance
___ 3. OBSTACLES   C. Fearlessness; boldness
___ 4. ACRID   D. Created; put together
___ 5. AUDACITY   E. Morally, socially, or legally obliged to another; beholden
___ 6. FLEETING   F. Made known something private or secret
___ 7. SUBSIDED   G. Lying in wait, as in ambush
___ 8. COUNTERED   H. Unpleasantly sharp, pungent, or bitter to smell
___ 9. STOICALLY   I. Disdainfully; scornfully
___10. RESOLUTION   J. Loss of soul; eternal damnation
___11. SCOFFED   K. Unaffected by pleasure or pain; impassively
___12. INDEBTED   L. Worried unease; anxiety
___13. INSTINCTIVELY   M. Things that oppose or stand in the way of
___14. CARAVAN   N. Company of travelers journeying together
___15. FURROW   O. Firm determination
___16. LURKING   P. Unresistingly accepting
___17. DIVULGED   Q. A rut, groove, or narrow depression
___18. CONTEMPTUOUSLY   R. Mocked or treated with derision
___19. RESIGNED   S. Wander in search of food or provisions
___20. PERDITION   T. Moving swiftly; rapid or nimble
___21. IMPENDING   U. Offered in response
___22. FORAGE   V. Done by innate aptitude
___23. DISQUIETUDE   W. Giving up something formerly held dear
___24. ARROGANT   X. Ghosts or apparitions
___25. WROUGHT   Y. Became less agitated or active

Bless Me Ultima Vocabulary Matching 3 Answer Key

W - 1.	FORSAKING	A.	About to take place
X - 2.	PHANTOMS	B.	Making claims to unwarranted importance
M - 3.	OBSTACLES	C.	Fearlessness; boldness
H - 4.	ACRID	D.	Created; put together
C - 5.	AUDACITY	E.	Morally, socially, or legally obliged to another; beholden
T - 6.	FLEETING	F.	Made known something private or secret
Y - 7.	SUBSIDED	G.	Lying in wait, as in ambush
U - 8.	COUNTERED	H.	Unpleasantly sharp, pungent, or bitter to smell
K - 9.	STOICALLY	I.	Disdainfully; scornfully
O - 10.	RESOLUTION	J.	Loss of soul; eternal damnation
R - 11.	SCOFFED	K.	Unaffected by pleasure or pain; impassively
E - 12.	INDEBTED	L.	Worried unease; anxiety
V - 13.	INSTINCTIVELY	M.	Things that oppose or stand in the way of
N - 14.	CARAVAN	N.	Company of travelers journeying together
Q - 15.	FURROW	O.	Firm determination
G - 16.	LURKING	P.	Unresistingly accepting
F - 17.	DIVULGED	Q.	A rut, groove, or narrow depression
I - 18.	CONTEMPTUOUSLY	R.	Mocked or treated with derision
P - 19.	RESIGNED	S.	Wander in search of food or provisions
J - 20.	PERDITION	T.	Moving swiftly; rapid or nimble
A - 21.	IMPENDING	U.	Offered in response
S - 22.	FORAGE	V.	Done by innate aptitude
L - 23.	DISQUIETUDE	W.	Giving up something formerly held dear
B - 24.	ARROGANT	X.	Ghosts or apparitions
D - 25.	WROUGHT	Y.	Became less agitated or active

Bless Me Ultima Vocabulary Matching 4

___ 1. SUCCULENT   A. Morally, socially, or legally obliged to another; beholden
___ 2. VAGABONDS   B. Pride; joy
___ 3. EMACIATED   C. Wander in search of food or provisions
___ 4. CONTEMPTUOUSLY   D. Done by innate aptitude
___ 5. ILLUMINATED   E. Trembled
___ 6. DEFIANCE   F. Made extremely thin, especially as a result of starvation
___ 7. INSTINCTIVELY   G. A rut, groove, or narrow depression
___ 8. ADMONISHED   H. Scornfully or cynically mocking
___ 9. MELEE   I. Violated the sacredness of; profaned
___10. INDEBTED   J. People without permanent homes
___11. ARROGANT   K. Unpleasantly sharp, pungent, or bitter to smell
___12. PERDITION   L. Lit up
___13. ACRID   M. Violent free-for-all
___14. DEBRIS   N. Rubble or wreckage
___15. SARDONICALLY   O. Made known something private or secret
___16. PULSATING   P. Joyous; full of high spirits
___17. DESECRATED   Q. Reproved gently but earnestly
___18. EXUBERANT   R. Making claims to unwarranted importance
___19. DIVULGED   S. Not disturbed or confused
___20. FORAGE   T. Full of juice or sap; juicy
___21. BRISTLED   U. Bold resistance
___22. ELATION   V. Caused to stand erect; stiffened
___23. QUAVERED   W. Loss of soul; eternal damnation
___24. UNPERTURBED   X. Expanding and contracting rhythmically; beating
___25. FURROW   Y. Disdainfully; scornfully

Bless Me Ultima Vocabulary Matching 4 Answer Key

T - 1. SUCCULENT	A. Morally, socially, or legally obliged to another; beholden
J - 2. VAGABONDS	B. Pride; joy
F - 3. EMACIATED	C. Wander in search of food or provisions
Y - 4. CONTEMPTUOUSLY	D. Done by innate aptitude
L - 5. ILLUMINATED	E. Trembled
U - 6. DEFIANCE	F. Made extremely thin, especially as a result of starvation
D - 7. INSTINCTIVELY	G. A rut, groove, or narrow depression
Q - 8. ADMONISHED	H. Scornfully or cynically mocking
M - 9. MELEE	I. Violated the sacredness of; profaned
A - 10. INDEBTED	J. People without permanent homes
R - 11. ARROGANT	K. Unpleasantly sharp, pungent, or bitter to smell
W - 12. PERDITION	L. Lit up
K - 13. ACRID	M. Violent free-for-all
N - 14. DEBRIS	N. Rubble or wreckage
H - 15. SARDONICALLY	O. Made known something private or secret
X - 16. PULSATING	P. Joyous; full of high spirits
I - 17. DESECRATED	Q. Reproved gently but earnestly
P - 18. EXUBERANT	R. Making claims to unwarranted importance
O - 19. DIVULGED	S. Not disturbed or confused
C - 20. FORAGE	T. Full of juice or sap; juicy
V - 21. BRISTLED	U. Bold resistance
B - 22. ELATION	V. Caused to stand erect; stiffened
E - 23. QUAVERED	W. Loss of soul; eternal damnation
S - 24. UNPERTURBED	X. Expanding and contracting rhythmically; beating
G - 25. FURROW	Y. Disdainfully; scornfully

Bless Me Ultima Vocabulary Magic Squares 1

Match the definition with the vocabulary word. Put your answers in the magic squares below. When your answers are correct, all columns and rows will add to the same number.

A. IRREVOCABLE
B. EMPHATICALLY
C. IMPENDING
D. MANIPULATED
E. DRONE
F. SUCCULENT
G. FURROW
H. ENDURES
I. LURKING
J. SUBSIDED
K. EMANATED
L. REVERBERATING
M. EXASPERATION
N. ABRUPTLY
O. OBSTACLES
P. ILLUMINATED

1. Suddenly
2. A rut, groove, or narrow depression
3. Resounding in a series of echoes
4. Impossible to retract or take back
5. Came forth or sent forth, as from a source
6. Positively; definitely
7. Anger or impatience
8. Continues in existence; lasts
9. Continuous, low, dull humming sound
10. Lit up
11. About to take place
12. Became less agitated or active
13. Influenced or managed shrewdly or deviously
14. Lying in wait, as in ambush
15. Full of juice or sap; juicy
16. Things that oppose or stand in the way of

A=	B=	C=	D=
E=	F=	G=	H=
I=	J=	K=	L=
M=	N=	O=	P=

Bless Me Ultima Vocabulary Magic Squares 1 Answer Key

Match the definition with the vocabulary word. Put your answers in the magic squares below. When your answers are correct, all columns and rows will add to the same number.

A. IRREVOCABLE
B. EMPHATICALLY
C. IMPENDING
D. MANIPULATED
E. DRONE
F. SUCCULENT
G. FURROW
H. ENDURES
I. LURKING
J. SUBSIDED
K. EMANATED
L. REVERBERATING
M. EXASPERATION
N. ABRUPTLY
O. OBSTACLES
P. ILLUMINATED

1. Suddenly
2. A rut, groove, or narrow depression
3. Resounding in a series of echoes
4. Impossible to retract or take back
5. Came forth or sent forth, as from a source
6. Positively; definitely
7. Anger or impatience
8. Continues in existence; lasts
9. Continuous, low, dull humming sound
10. Lit up
11. About to take place
12. Became less agitated or active
13. Influenced or managed shrewdly or deviously
14. Lying in wait, as in ambush
15. Full of juice or sap; juicy
16. Things that oppose or stand in the way of

A=4	B=6	C=11	D=13
E=9	F=15	G=2	H=8
I=14	J=12	K=5	L=3
M=7	N=1	O=16	P=10

Bless Me Ultima Vocabulary Magic Squares 2

Match the definition with the vocabulary word. Put your answers in the magic squares below. When your answers are correct, all columns and rows will add to the same number.

A. WROUGHT
B. RESIGNED
C. DRONE
D. CROONED
E. INTERMINABLE
F. INSTINCTIVELY
G. ILLUMINATED
H. INDEBTED
I. BLEMISH
J. TORMENTED
K. EMACIATED
L. FORSAKING
M. INCANTATION
N. DESECRATED
O. DISQUIETUDE
P. SCOFFED

1. Worried unease; anxiety
2. Sung softly or in a humming way
3. Caused great pain or anguish
4. Endless
5. Imperfection that mars or impairs
6. Done by innate aptitude
7. Mocked or treated with derision
8. Continuous, low, dull humming sound
9. Morally, socially, or legally obliged to another; beholden
10. Made extremely thin, especially as a result of starvation
11. Created; put together
12. Violated the sacredness of; profaned
13. Unresistingly accepting
14. Ritual recitation of charms or spells to produce magic
15. Lit up
16. Giving up something formerly held dear

A=	B=	C=	D=
E=	F=	G=	H=
I=	J=	K=	L=
M=	N=	O=	P=

Bless Me Ultima Vocabulary Magic Squares 2 Answer Key

Match the definition with the vocabulary word. Put your answers in the magic squares below. When your answers are correct, all columns and rows will add to the same number.

A. WROUGHT
B. RESIGNED
C. DRONE
D. CROONED
E. INTERMINABLE
F. INSTINCTIVELY
G. ILLUMINATED
H. INDEBTED
I. BLEMISH
J. TORMENTED
K. EMACIATED
L. FORSAKING
M. INCANTATION
N. DESECRATED
O. DISQUIETUDE
P. SCOFFED

1. Worried unease; anxiety
2. Sung softly or in a humming way
3. Caused great pain or anguish
4. Endless
5. Imperfection that mars or impairs
6. Done by innate aptitude
7. Mocked or treated with derision
8. Continuous, low, dull humming sound
9. Morally, socially, or legally obliged to another; beholden
10. Made extremely thin, especially as a result of starvation
11. Created; put together
12. Violated the sacredness of; profaned
13. Unresistingly accepting
14. Ritual recitation of charms or spells to produce magic
15. Lit up
16. Giving up something formerly held dear

A=11	B=13	C=8	D=2
E=4	F=6	G=15	H=9
I=5	J=3	K=10	L=16
M=14	N=12	O=1	P=7

Bless Me Ultima Vocabulary Magic Squares 3

Match the definition with the vocabulary word. Put your answers in the magic squares below. When your answers are correct, all columns and rows will add to the same number.

A. ILLUMINATED
B. RESOLUTION
C. STOICALLY
D. ENDOWED
E. EXORCISE
F. LURKING
G. ETCHED
H. ENDURES
I. PULSATING
J. ADMONISHED
K. WROUGHT
L. SUBSIDED
M. SARDONICALLY
N. EMACIATED
O. FLEETING
P. BRISTLED

1. Scornfully or cynically mocking
2. Lying in wait, as in ambush
3. Continues in existence; lasts
4. Moving swiftly; rapid or nimble
5. Became less agitated or active
6. Unaffected by pleasure or pain; impassively
7. Lit up
8. Reproved gently but earnestly
9. Created; put together
10. Provided with property or income
11. Firm determination
12. Expanding and contracting rhythmically; beating
13. Made extremely thin, especially as a result of starvation
14. Free from evil spirits or malign influences
15. Cut into the surface of
16. Caused to stand erect; stiffened

A= 7	B= 11	C= 6	D= 10
E= 14	F= 2	G= 15	H= 3
I= 12	J= 8	K= 9	L= 5
M= 1	N= 13	O= 4	P= 16

Bless Me Ultima Vocabulary Magic Squares 3 Answer Key

Match the definition with the vocabulary word. Put your answers in the magic squares below. When your answers are correct, all columns and rows will add to the same number.

A. ILLUMINATED
B. RESOLUTION
C. STOICALLY
D. ENDOWED
E. EXORCISE
F. LURKING
G. ETCHED
H. ENDURES
I. PULSATING
J. ADMONISHED
K. WROUGHT
L. SUBSIDED
M. SARDONICALLY
N. EMACIATED
O. FLEETING
P. BRISTLED

1. Scornfully or cynically mocking
2. Lying in wait, as in ambush
3. Continues in existence; lasts
4. Moving swiftly; rapid or nimble
5. Became less agitated or active
6. Unaffected by pleasure or pain; impassively
7. Lit up
8. Reproved gently but earnestly
9. Created; put together
10. Provided with property or income
11. Firm determination
12. Expanding and contracting rhythmically; beating
13. Made extremely thin, especially as a result of starvation
14. Free from evil spirits or malign influences
15. Cut into the surface of
16. Caused to stand erect; stiffened

A=7	B=11	C=6	D=10
E=14	F=2	G=15	H=3
I=12	J=8	K=9	L=5
M=1	N=13	O=4	P=16

Bless Me Ultima Vocabulary Magic Squares 4

Match the definition with the vocabulary word. Put your answers in the magic squares below. When your answers are correct, all columns and rows will add to the same number.

A. PULSATING
B. INCANTATION
C. CONTEMPTUOUSLY
D. ENDURES
E. DISQUIETUDE
F. TRANSFIXED
G. ENDOWED
H. CARAVAN
I. EXUBERANT
J. INSTINCTIVELY
K. IMPENDING
L. IRREVOCABLE
M. BRISTLED
N. DIVULGED
O. PERDITION
P. EMACIATED

1. Rendered motionless, as with terror or amazement
2. Joyous; full of high spirits
3. Loss of soul; eternal damnation
4. Continues in existence; lasts
5. Caused to stand erect; stiffened
6. Ritual recitation of charms or spells to produce magic
7. Company of travelers journeying together
8. About to take place
9. Disdainfully; scornfully
10. Made extremely thin, especially as a result of starvation
11. Done by innate aptitude
12. Worried unease; anxiety
13. Impossible to retract or take back
14. Provided with property or income
15. Expanding and contracting rhythmically; beating
16. Made known something private or secret

A=	B=	C=	D=
E=	F=	G=	H=
I=	J=	K=	L=
M=	N=	O=	P=

Bless Me Ultima Vocabulary Magic Squares 4 Answer Key

Match the definition with the vocabulary word. Put your answers in the magic squares below. When your answers are correct, all columns and rows will add to the same number.

A. PULSATING
B. INCANTATION
C. CONTEMPTUOUSLY
D. ENDURES
E. DISQUIETUDE
F. TRANSFIXED
G. ENDOWED
H. CARAVAN
I. EXUBERANT
J. INSTINCTIVELY
K. IMPENDING
L. IRREVOCABLE
M. BRISTLED
N. DIVULGED
O. PERDITION
P. EMACIATED

1. Rendered motionless, as with terror or amazement
2. Joyous; full of high spirits
3. Loss of soul; eternal damnation
4. Continues in existence; lasts
5. Caused to stand erect; stiffened
6. Ritual recitation of charms or spells to produce magic
7. Company of travelers journeying together
8. About to take place
9. Disdainfully; scornfully
10. Made extremely thin, especially as a result of starvation
11. Done by innate aptitude
12. Worried unease; anxiety
13. Impossible to retract or take back
14. Provided with property or income
15. Expanding and contracting rhythmically; beating
16. Made known something private or secret

A=15	B=6	C=9	D=4
E=12	F=1	G=14	H=7
I=2	J=11	K=8	L=13
M=5	N=16	O=3	P=10

Bless Me Ultima Vocabulary Word Search 1

```
Z V F O R A G E W S X C D E L T S I R B
M A S T W F J O V M G I R Q Z I S T B Y
W G C D R T R W B X R D P O R E H L G R
Y A J O O R Z X Y C M D N B O C T C D N
S B E X U B E R A N T Y E M A N A T E D
E O S F G N B S Q R R D U N O A E W D C
R N S Y H B T X U E R N P I J I H D I S
E D Q T T A P E T C P O T Y G F S S S T
H S I M E L B N R E C I G E R E S T B H
Z E E M W N E R R E D U S A T D R U U H
S L N Y E S A T U R D I L C N N P P S L
M C D E Y L U C E P C I H E S T C O U V
O A O D L R E P I R T E V E N D U R E S
T T W F B A S E O O D L N U K T K V Z Y
E S E E F C T X K S U O Y T L I P T Q L
S B D R Z E E I X R S D E N G I S E R
B O T D V C D B O D S X L G J D E H J F
P V F O R S A K I N G C H Y Q D R D D Z
```

A rut, groove, or narrow depression (6)
Became less agitated or active (8)
Bold resistance (8)
Came forth or sent forth, as from a source (8)
Cases for sword or knife blades (7)
Caused to stand erect; stiffened (8)
Continues in existence; lasts (7)
Continuous, low, dull humming sound (5)
Created; put together (7)
Cut into the surface of (6)
Dissension from dogma by a professed believer (6)
Free from evil spirits or malign influences (8)
Full of juice or sap; juicy (9)
Giving up something formerly held dear (9)
Imperfection that mars or impairs (7)
Inflammatory disorder of the lower intestinal tract (9)
Joyous; full of high spirits (9)
Loss of soul; eternal damnation (9)
Lying in wait, as in ambush (7)
Made known something private or secret (8)
Making claims to unwarranted importance (8)
Mocked or treated with derision (7)
Not disturbed or confused (11)
Offered in response (9)
People without permanent homes (9)
Persistently (11)
Pride; joy (7)
Provided with property or income (7)
Rubble or wreckage (6)
State of mental numbness; a daze (6)
Suddenly (8)
Sung softly or in a humming way (7)
Things that oppose or stand in the way of (9)
Unpleasantly sharp, pungent, or bitter to smell (5)
Unresistingly accepting (8)
Very small particles; specks (5)
Violent free-for-all (5)
Wander in search of food or provisions (6)

Bless Me Ultima Vocabulary Word Search 1 Answer Key

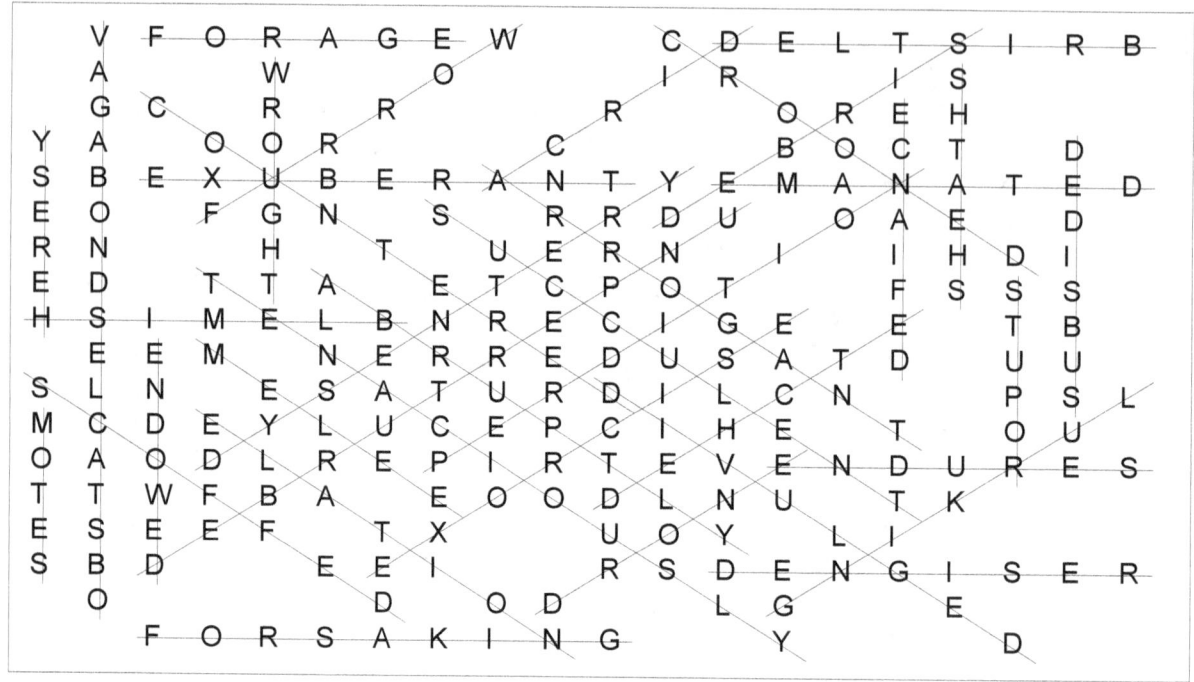

A rut, groove, or narrow depression (6)
Became less agitated or active (8)
Bold resistance (8)
Came forth or sent forth, as from a source (8)
Cases for sword or knife blades (7)
Caused to stand erect; stiffened (8)
Continues in existence; lasts (7)
Continuous, low, dull humming sound (5)
Created; put together (7)
Cut into the surface of (6)
Dissension from dogma by a professed believer (6)
Free from evil spirits or malign influences (8)
Full of juice or sap; juicy (9)
Giving up something formerly held dear (9)
Imperfection that mars or impairs (7)
Inflammatory disorder of the lower intestinal tract (9)
Joyous; full of high spirits (9)
Loss of soul; eternal damnation (9)
Lying in wait, as in ambush (7)
Made known something private or secret (8)
Making claims to unwarranted importance (8)
Mocked or treated with derision (7)
Not disturbed or confused (11)
Offered in response (9)
People without permanent homes (9)
Persistently (11)

Pride; joy (7)
Provided with property or income (7)
Rubble or wreckage (6)
State of mental numbness; a daze (6)
Suddenly (8)
Sung softly or in a humming way (7)
Things that oppose or stand in the way of (9)
Unpleasantly sharp, pungent, or bitter to smell (5)
Unresistingly accepting (8)
Very small particles; specks (5)
Violent free-for-all (5)
Wander in search of food or provisions (6)

Bless Me Ultima Vocabulary Word Search 2

```
S Z S D S M O T N A H P C L A M O R E D
C N T A K H N R W R O U G H T F U S Y Y
O Y U T R A E C R O O N E D S N I L T G
F Y P H G D S A G L I X X H P C L N C
F L O O E C O H T K W Z Y E R A C I M B
E W R H G L Y N A H J G R O C A D S C H
D R C P A B A S I T S T X I D N U W O S
A T Z E R X R T R C U E T U E C O Y U R
E Y C R O O L A I R A A A P C R T P N K
R S H D F P N M B O H L M U R X M S T D
Z E W I N S Q E Q P N I L U A O C U E T
D R S T F X D L M E E E F Y T C A B R F
D E F I A N C E M A N A T E D Z R S E W
P H X O G X R E Q T D D S F Z I A I D T
Y E K N X N D X D L U R O X S L V D D L
D E T A R C E S E D R S O W J P A E L Y
I N D E B T E D X L E F S N E D N D H Q
B L E M I S H Y S X S T S H E D V F V S
```

A rut, groove, or narrow depression (6)
About to take place (9)
Became less agitated or active (8)
Bold resistance (8)
Came forth or sent forth, as from a source (8)
Cases for sword or knife blades (7)
Company of travelers journeying together (7)
Continues in existence; lasts (7)
Continuous, low, dull humming sound (5)
Created; put together (7)
Cut into the surface of (6)
Dissension from dogma by a professed believer (6)
Fearlessness; boldness (8)
Free from evil spirits or malign influences (8)
Full of juice or sap; juicy (9)
Ghosts or apparitions (8)
Giving up something formerly held dear (9)
Imperfection that mars or impairs (7)
Loss of soul; eternal damnation (9)
Made a loud, sustained noise or outcry (8)
Making claims to unwarranted importance (8)
Mocked or treated with derision (7)
Morally, socially, or legally obliged to another; beholden (8)
Not disturbed or confused (11)
Offered in response (9)
Positively; definitely (12)

Pride; joy (7)
Provided with property or income (7)
Rendered motionless, as with terror or amazement (10)
Rubble or wreckage (6)
Scornfully or cynically mocking (12)
State of mental numbness; a daze (6)
Sung softly or in a humming way (7)
Unpleasantly sharp, pungent, or bitter to smell (5)
Unresistingly accepting (8)
Very small particles; specks (5)
Violated the sacredness of; profaned (10)
Violent free-for-all (5)
Wander in search of food or provisions (6)

Bless Me Ultima Vocabulary Word Search 2 Answer Key

```
S       S     S M O T N A H P C L A M O R E D
C     T A     H N   W R O U G H T     U S Y Y
O     U R A E C R O O N E D     N I L T G
F     P G D   A     I       P C L I N
F     O O E O   T K       E R A C I
E     R H G L   N A H     R O C A D S C
D R C P A   A S I T S T X I D N U W O
A T   E R   R T R C U E T U E C O   U
E Y   R O O A I R A A P C R       N
R S   D F   N M B O H L M U R   M S   D
  E   I   S   E P N I L A O C U E
  R S T F   D L M E E F Y T C A B R
D E F I A N C E M A N A T E D   R S E
  H X O G     E   T D D S     I A I D
  E   N N       U R O   S     V D D
D E T A R C E S E D R     O W     A E
I N D E B T E D         E       N E N D
B L E M I S H           S       E D
```

A rut, groove, or narrow depression (6)
About to take place (9)
Became less agitated or active (8)
Bold resistance (8)
Came forth or sent forth, as from a source (8)
Cases for sword or knife blades (7)
Company of travelers journeying together (7)
Continues in existence; lasts (7)
Continuous, low, dull humming sound (5)
Created; put together (7)
Cut into the surface of (6)
Dissension from dogma by a professed believer (6)
Fearlessness; boldness (8)
Free from evil spirits or malign influences (8)
Full of juice or sap; juicy (9)
Ghosts or apparitions (8)
Giving up something formerly held dear (9)
Imperfection that mars or impairs (7)
Loss of soul; eternal damnation (9)
Made a loud, sustained noise or outcry (8)
Making claims to unwarranted importance (8)
Mocked or treated with derision (7)
Morally, socially, or legally obliged to another; beholden (8)
Not disturbed or confused (11)
Offered in response (9)
Positively; definitely (12)
Pride; joy (7)
Provided with property or income (7)
Rendered motionless, as with terror or amazement (10)
Rubble or wreckage (6)
Scornfully or cynically mocking (12)
State of mental numbness; a daze (6)
Sung softly or in a humming way (7)
Unpleasantly sharp, pungent, or bitter to smell (5)
Unresistingly accepting (8)
Very small particles; specks (5)
Violated the sacredness of; profaned (10)
Violent free-for-all (5)
Wander in search of food or provisions (6)

Bless Me Ultima Vocabulary Word Search 3

```
M T I N C A N T A T I O N F Y S E R E H
S O C D Y S E N T E R Y O U P U T P P M
J C T L U R K I N G R R I R Q B J Y F D
C N O E D E N G I S E R T R C S R H G N
D O L F S B D D H B V H A O Q I H V D R
K I M T F B R T C W O R L W V D M N E R
N T F M R E A I L B C Z E I P E S O B J
W U O G O E D C S D A P G D X D T I R Q
G L R G H T D Z C T B I E E W J U S I N
N O A S T O I C A L L Y Z R B K P U S S
I S G Z B C M O Q A E E O E D H O R X N
D E E Z D P E F N X X U D T A I R T Z X
N R M L H N L T Z T G I Q N Q E T N Q Y
E C T A O Q E C L H N C T U X R N I T Z
P N R R C S E R T D V O E O A A Y I O F
M D D O F I D X E M M T R C V V C Y K N
I Q G U O I A B Z S C C W A S A E R S D
R R W J R N T T Y H I D R K D B S R C D
J M Q C V E E H E S J A N U Y N H D E P
D C A X D S S D E D C M A E N D O W E D
```

ACRID	DRONE	FORAGE	LURKING	SCOFFED
AUDACITY	DYSENTERY	FURROW	MELEE	SHEATHS
BRISTLED	ELATION	HERESY	MOTES	STOICALLY
CARAVAN	EMACIATED	IMPENDING	PERDITION	STUPOR
COMMOTION	ENDOWED	INCANTATION	PHANTOMS	SUBSIDED
COUNTERED	ENDURES	INDEBTED	QUAVERED	VIGILANTES
CROONED	ETCHED	INTRUSION	RESIGNED	WROUGHT
DEBRIS	EXORCISE	IRREVOCABLE	RESOLUTION	

Bless Me Ultima Vocabulary Word Search 3 Answer Key

```
M     I  N  C  A  N  T  A  T  I  O  N     F     Y     S  E  R  E  H
S  O     D  Y  S  E  N  T  E  R  Y     O        U
   C  T  L  U  R  K  I  N  G  R        I  R     B
C  N  O  E  D  E  N  G  I  S  E  R     T  R     S
   O     F  S  B        H     V     R  A  O     I           D
   I  M     F     R  T        O        L  W  V  D        N  E
   T  F  M     E  A  I        C        E     I     D     O  B
   U  O     O  E  D        S     A  P  G  D  E     S     I  R
G  L  R     H  T        T     B  I  E     W     U     S
   O  A  S  T  O  I  C  A  L  L  Y  R  O  E  D  H     R
N  S  G     M        A  E  E     D  A     I     O     T
I  E     M        E     N     U  D  N  T  E     R     N
D  R        N  L  T        G  I  Q     X     N     N     Y
N  C     A  O  E        H  N     T  U  X  A     I        T
E  N  R  R  C  S     T  D     O  E  O  A  A     O        O
P     D  O  I  D     E     M  T  R  C  V  V  C        N
M        U  O  I  A  B     S  C  C  A     A  E
I           R  N  T  T     H  I           R        D        R
            C     E  E     E  S        A  U              E
         A  D        S  D  E  D  C     A  E  N  D  O  W  E  D
```

ACRID	DRONE	FORAGE	LURKING	SCOFFED
AUDACITY	DYSENTERY	FURROW	MELEE	SHEATHS
BRISTLED	ELATION	HERESY	MOTES	STOICALLY
CARAVAN	EMACIATED	IMPENDING	PERDITION	STUPOR
COMMOTION	ENDOWED	INCANTATION	PHANTOMS	SUBSIDED
COUNTERED	ENDURES	INDEBTED	QUAVERED	VIGILANTES
CROONED	ETCHED	INTRUSION	RESIGNED	WROUGHT
DEBRIS	EXORCISE	IRREVOCABLE	RESOLUTION	

Bless Me Ultima Vocabulary Word Search 4

```
A B R U P T L Y I M P E N D I N G E E J
A P E C S P Y X F R T O K W D N E L N G
D D S M Z W T W N C I T E E Q L C B D M
M R I K H S K A H T D Y T N E T E A O M
O A G V P Y V E A T E A Y M D P G C W Z
N B N P U A D L K R N P H N C U A O E T
I L E I R L E N F A O X U J Y I R V D W
S E D A P V G Q M N O J H L W N O E N C
H M C W Y U Y E G S R P S X S C F R S R
E I B F X D L H D F C G T C J A M R O Z
D S W K T E C A P I S F U D G N T I N Z
E H G G P T J T T X D C P N S T T Z Q
T R T S U B S I D E D F O R S A K I N G
A T H N G E X Y L D D I R M R T C W Z G
R J G X W D F T B J S T D E M I B C F F
C G U Y Q N S Z D U H M P E D O F J U N
E X O R C I S E R H S S O I B N T F R M
S Q R J R G Y T O K A K R T G R L I R Z
E X W B H K N F N X P C S S E M I Q O X
D L U R K I N G E R A H E R E S Y S W N
```

ABRUPTLY	DEBRIS	ETCHED	INCANTATION	PULSATING
ACRID	DESECRATED	EXASPERATION	INDEBTED	RESIGNED
ADMONISHED	DIVULGED	EXORCISE	INTRUSION	STUPOR
BLEMISH	DRONE	FORAGE	IRREVOCABLE	SUBSIDED
BRISTLED	ELATION	FORSAKING	LURKING	TRANSFIXED
CARAVAN	EMANATED	FURROW	MANIPULATED	WROUGHT
COMMOTION	ENDOWED	HERESY	MELEE	
CROONED	ENDURES	IMPENDING	MOTES	

Bless Me Ultima Vocabulary Word Search 4 Answer Key

ABRUPTLY	DEBRIS	ETCHED	INCANTATION	PULSATING
ACRID	DESECRATED	EXASPERATION	INDEBTED	RESIGNED
ADMONISHED	DIVULGED	EXORCISE	INTRUSION	STUPOR
BLEMISH	DRONE	FORAGE	IRREVOCABLE	SUBSIDED
BRISTLED	ELATION	FORSAKING	LURKING	TRANSFIXED
CARAVAN	EMANATED	FURROW	MANIPULATED	WROUGHT
COMMOTION	ENDOWED	HERESY	MELEE	
CROONED	ENDURES	IMPENDING	MOTES	

Bless Me Ultima Vocabulary Crossword 1

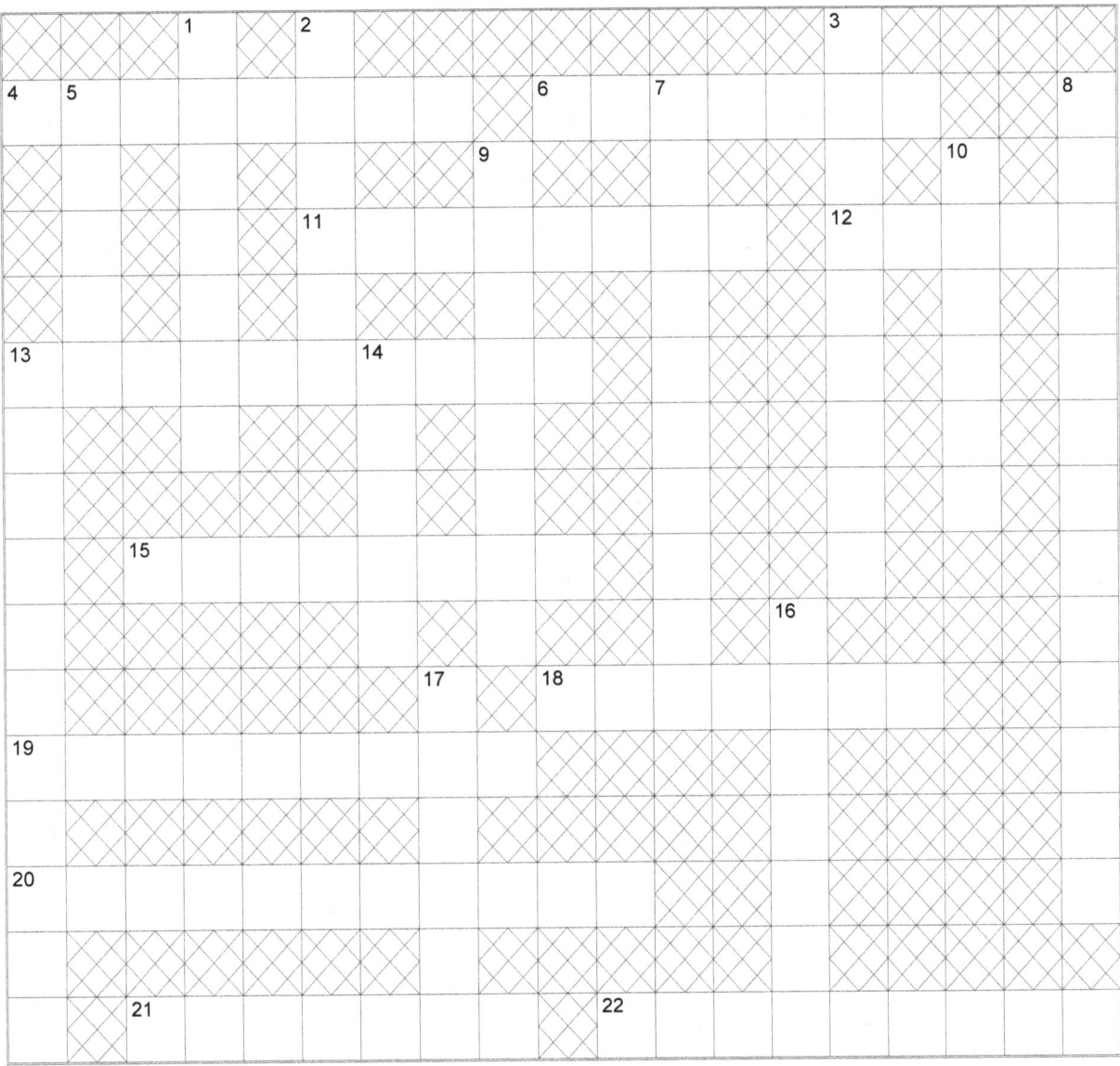

Across
4. Came forth or sent forth, as from a source
6. Pride; joy
11. Ghosts or apparitions
12. Very small particles; specks
13. Violated the sacredness of; profaned
15. Became less agitated or active
18. Continues in existence; lasts
19. Made extremely thin, especially as a result of starvation
20. Not disturbed or confused
21. Imperfection that mars or impairs
22. Things that oppose or stand in the way of

Down
1. Provided with property or income
2. State of mental numbness; a daze
3. Caused great pain or anguish
5. Violent free-for-all
7. Reproved gently but earnestly
8. Done by innate aptitude
9. Morally, socially, or legally obliged to another; beholden
10. Cut into the surface of
13. Worried unease; anxiety
14. Unpleasantly sharp, pungent, or bitter to smell
16. Created; put together
17. Rubble or wreckage

Bless Me Ultima Vocabulary Crossword 1 Answer Key

			1 E		2 S						3 T			
4 E	5 M	A	N	A	T	E	D		6 E	7 L	A	T	I	O	N		8 I
	E		D		U			9 I		A			D		R		10 E		N
	L		O		11 P	H	A	N	T	O	M	S		12 M	O	T	E	S
	E		W		O			D		O				E		C		T
13 D	E	S	E	C	R	A	14 T	E	D		N			N		H		I
I			D				C		B		I			T		E		N
S							R		T		S			E		D		C
Q		15 S	U	B	S	I	D	E	D		H			D				T
U						D		D			E		16 W				I
I					17 D		18 E	N	D	U	R	E	S				V
19 E	M	A	C	I	A	T	E	D					O				E
T					B								U				L
20 U	N	P	E	R	T	U	R	B	E	D			G				Y
D					I								H				
E		21 B	L	E	M	I	S	H		22 O	B	S	T	A	C	L	E	S

Across
4. Came forth or sent forth, as from a source
6. Pride; joy
11. Ghosts or apparitions
12. Very small particles; specks
13. Violated the sacredness of; profaned
15. Became less agitated or active
18. Continues in existence; lasts
19. Made extremely thin, especially as a result of starvation
20. Not disturbed or confused
21. Imperfection that mars or impairs
22. Things that oppose or stand in the way of

9. Morally, socially, or legally obliged to another; beholden
10. Cut into the surface of
13. Worried unease; anxiety
14. Unpleasantly sharp, pungent, or bitter to smell
16. Created; put together
17. Rubble or wreckage

Down
1. Provided with property or income
2. State of mental numbness; a daze
3. Caused great pain or anguish
5. Violent free-for-all
7. Reproved gently but earnestly
8. Done by innate aptitude

Bless Me Ultima Vocabulary Crossword 2

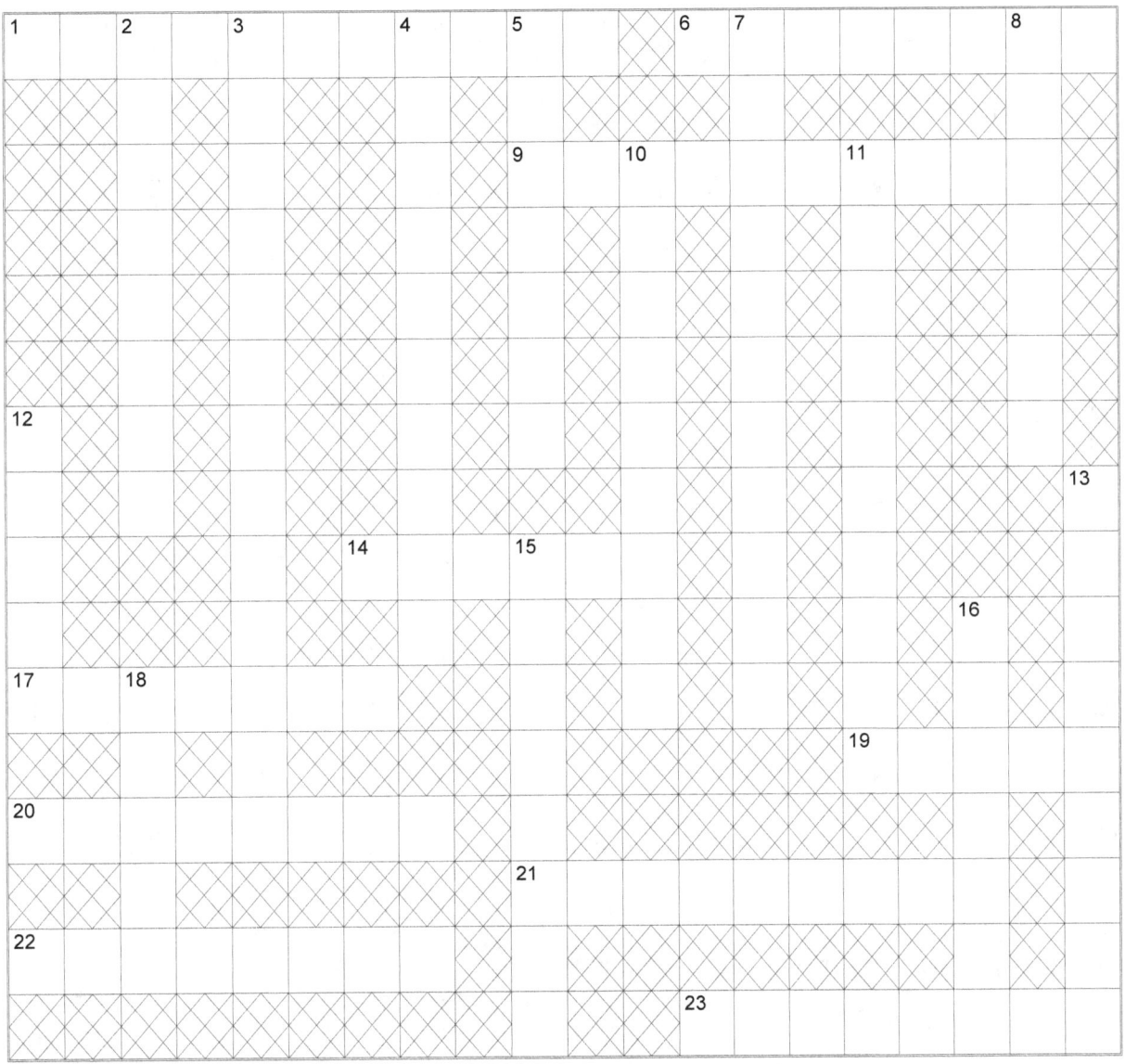

Across
1. Not disturbed or confused
6. Made known something private or secret
9. Violated the sacredness of; profaned
14. Wander in search of food or provisions
17. Pride; joy
19. Continuous, low, dull humming sound
20. Making claims to unwarranted importance
21. About to take place
22. Morally, socially, or legally obliged to another; beholden
23. Came forth or sent forth, as from a source

Down
2. Ghosts or apparitions
3. Resounding in a series of echoes
4. Firm determination
5. Provided with property or income
7. Ritual recitation of charms or spells to produce magic
8. Continues in existence; lasts
10. Full of juice or sap; juicy
11. Reproved gently but earnestly
12. Violent free-for-all
13. Caused great pain or anguish
15. Fearlessness; boldness
16. Created; put together
18. Unpleasantly sharp, pungent, or bitter to smell

Bless Me Ultima Vocabulary Crossword 2 Answer Key

	1 U	2 N	3 P	E	R	4 T	U	R	5 B	E	D		6 D	7 I	V	U	L	G	8 E	D
			H		E				E		N			N					N	
			A		V				9 D	10 E	S	E	C	R	11 A	T	E	D	
			N		E				O	O		U		A		D			U	
			T		R				L	W		C		N		M			R	
			O		B				U	E		C		T		O			E	
12 M	M		E						T	D		U		A		N			S	
E	S		R						I			L		T		I			13 T
L			A		14 F	O	R	15 A	G	E				I		S			O
E			T		N			U		N				O		H		16 W	R
17 E	18 L	A	T	I	O	N		D		T				N		E		R	M
	C		N					A								19 D	R	O	N	E
20 A	R	R	O	G	A	N	T			C							U		N
		I						21 I	M	P	E	N	D	I	N	G		T
22 I	N	D	E	B	T	E	D		T								H		E
								23 Y		E	M	A	N	A	T	E	D

Across
1. Not disturbed or confused
6. Made known something private or secret
9. Violated the sacredness of; profaned
14. Wander in search of food or provisions
17. Pride; joy
19. Continuous, low, dull humming sound
20. Making claims to unwarranted importance
21. About to take place
22. Morally, socially, or legally obliged to another; beholden
23. Came forth or sent forth, as from a source

Down
2. Ghosts or apparitions
3. Resounding in a series of echoes
4. Firm determination
5. Provided with property or income
7. Ritual recitation of charms or spells to produce magic
8. Continues in existence; lasts
10. Full of juice or sap; juicy
11. Reproved gently but earnestly
12. Violent free-for-all
13. Caused great pain or anguish
15. Fearlessness; boldness
16. Created; put together
18. Unpleasantly sharp, pungent, or bitter to smell

Bless Me Ultima Vocabulary Crossword 3

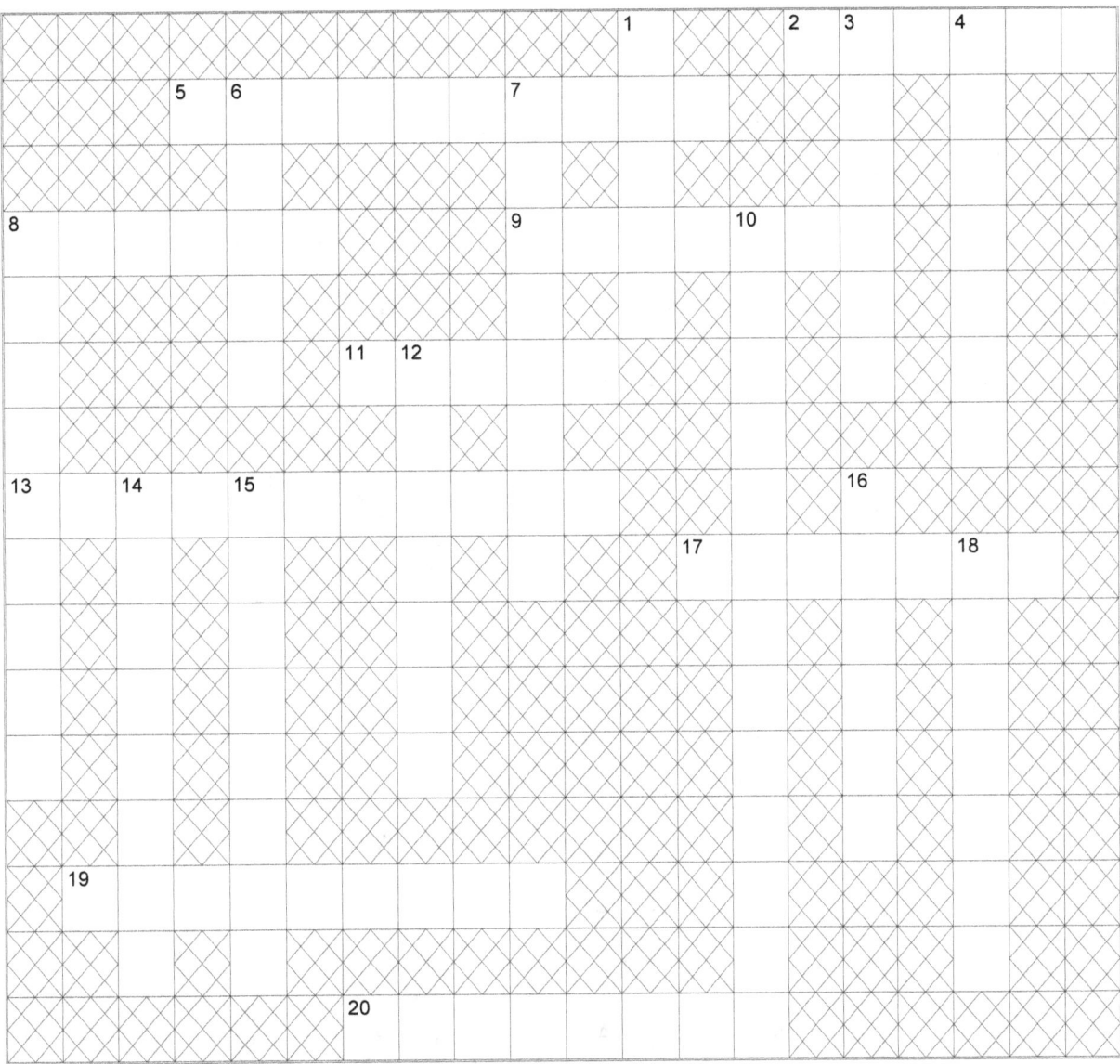

Across
2. Dissension from dogma by a professed believer
5. Reproved gently but earnestly
8. State of mental numbness; a daze
9. Imperfection that mars or impairs
11. Unpleasantly sharp, pungent, or bitter to smell
13. Not disturbed or confused
17. Continues in existence; lasts
19. About to take place
20. Fearlessness; boldness

Down
1. Violent free-for-all
3. Cut into the surface of
4. Provided with property or income
6. Continuous, low, dull humming sound
7. Became less agitated or active
8. Full of juice or sap; juicy
10. Done by innate aptitude
12. Company of travelers journeying together
14. Ghosts or apparitions
15. Unresistingly accepting
16. A rut, groove, or narrow depression
18. Pride; joy

Bless Me Ultima Vocabulary Crossword 3 Answer Key

Across
2. Dissension from dogma by a professed believer
5. Reproved gently but earnestly
8. State of mental numbness; a daze
9. Imperfection that mars or impairs
11. Unpleasantly sharp, pungent, or bitter to smell
13. Not disturbed or confused
17. Continues in existence; lasts
19. About to take place
20. Fearlessness; boldness

Down
1. Violent free-for-all
3. Cut into the surface of
4. Provided with property or income
6. Continuous, low, dull humming sound
7. Became less agitated or active
8. Full of juice or sap; juicy
10. Done by innate aptitude
12. Company of travelers journeying together
14. Ghosts or apparitions
15. Unresistingly accepting
16. A rut, groove, or narrow depression
18. Pride; joy

Bless Me Ultima Vocabulary Crossword 4

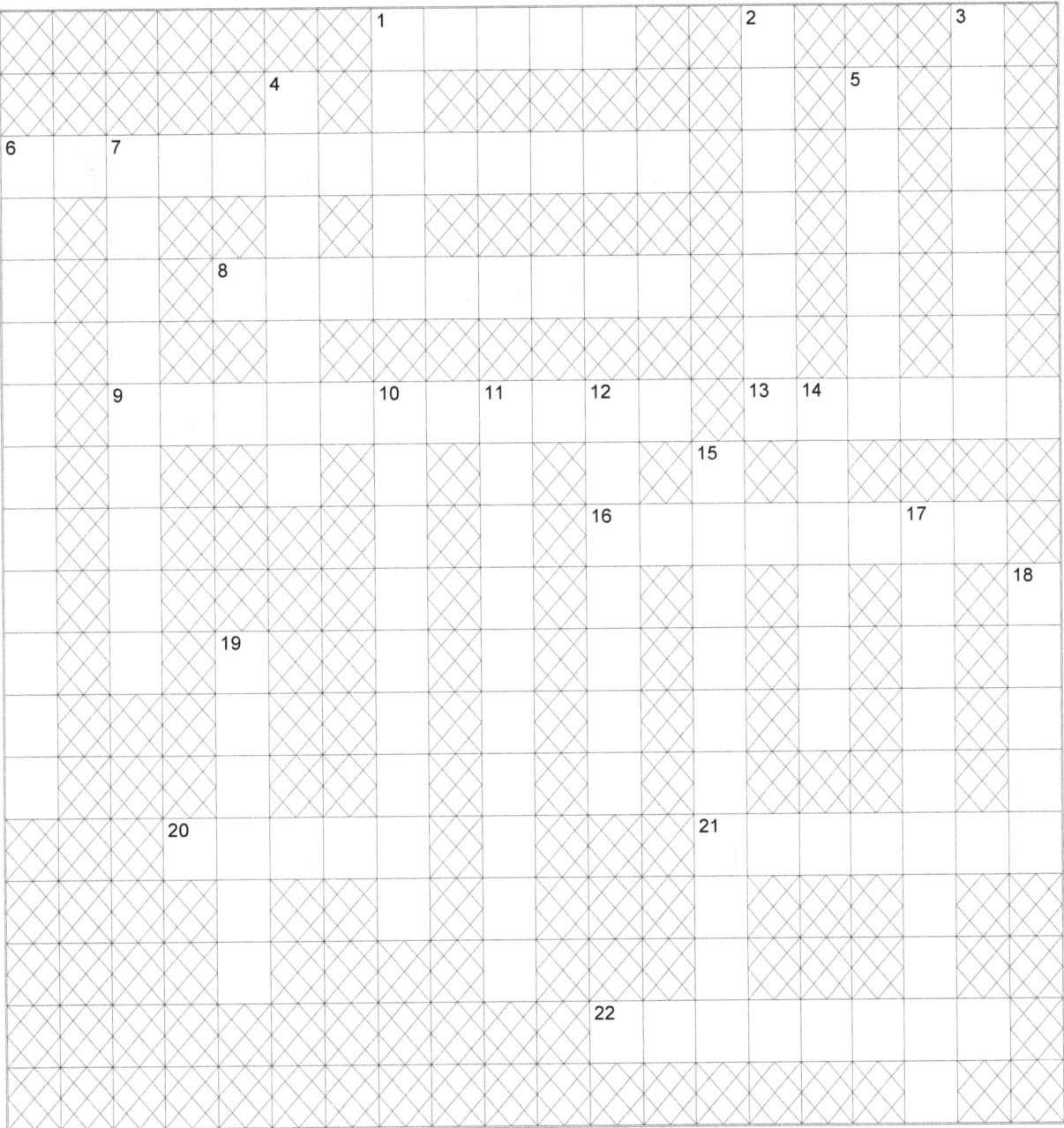

Across
1. Violent free-for-all
6. Done by innate aptitude
8. Giving up something formerly held dear
9. Not disturbed or confused
13. Dissension from dogma by a professed believer
16. Fearlessness; boldness
20. Continuous, low, dull humming sound
21. Mocked or treated with derision
22. Morally, socially, or legally obliged to another; beholden

Down
1. Very small particles; specks
2. Imperfection that mars or impairs
3. Continues in existence; lasts
4. Provided with property or income
5. State of mental numbness; a daze
6. Ritual recitation of charms or spells to produce magic
7. Full of juice or sap; juicy
10. Caused great pain or anguish
11. Firm determination
12. Pride; joy
14. Cut into the surface of
15. Reproved gently but earnestly
17. Rendered motionless, as with terror or amazement
18. Unpleasantly sharp, pungent, or bitter to smell
19. A rut, groove, or narrow depression

Bless Me Ultima Vocabulary Crossword 4 Answer Key

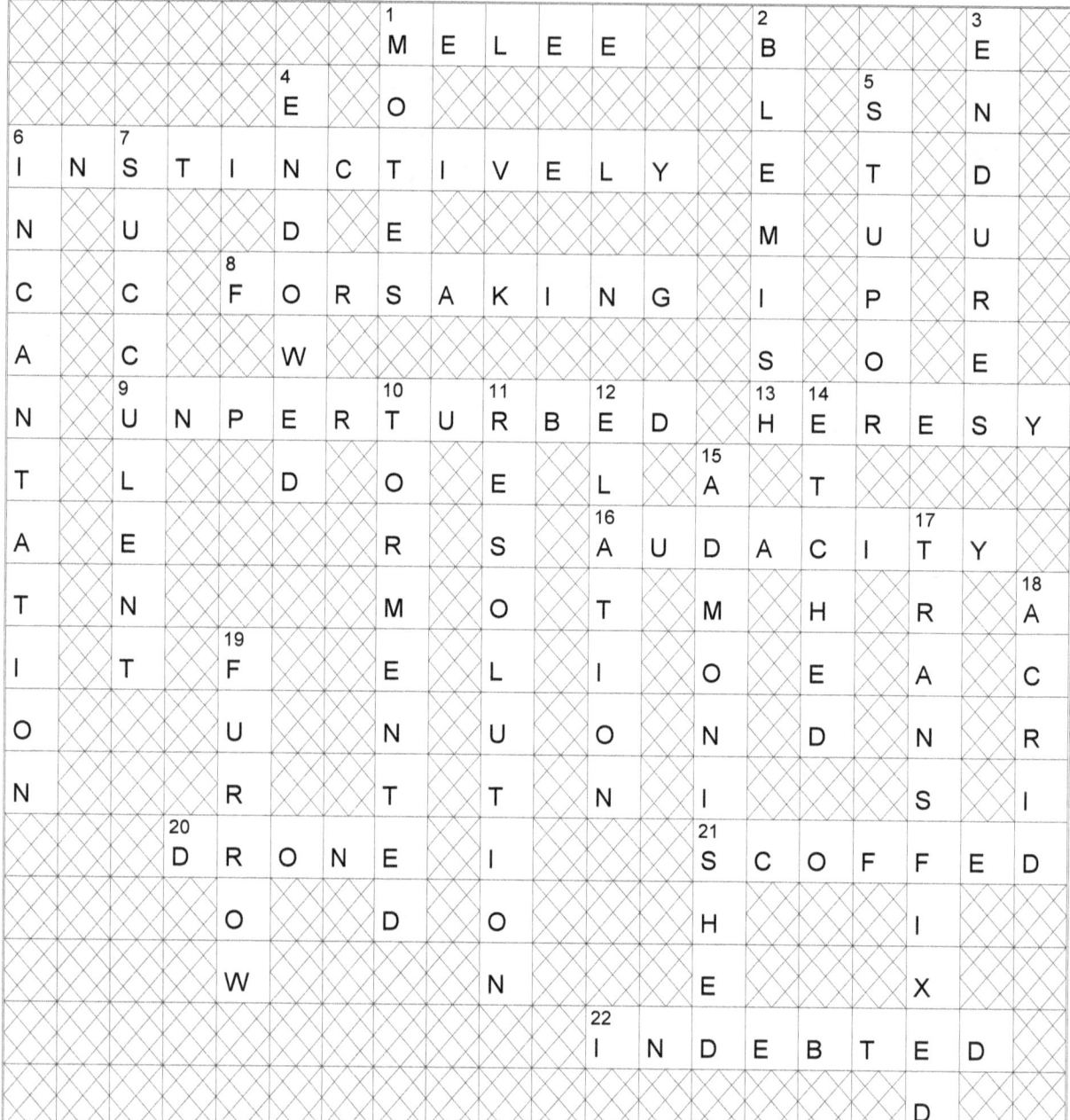

Across
1. Violent free-for-all
6. Done by innate aptitude
8. Giving up something formerly held dear
9. Not disturbed or confused
13. Dissension from dogma by a professed believer
16. Fearlessness; boldness
20. Continuous, low, dull humming sound
21. Mocked or treated with derision
22. Morally, socially, or legally obliged to another; beholden

Down
1. Very small particles; specks
2. Imperfection that mars or impairs
3. Continues in existence; lasts
4. Provided with property or income
5. State of mental numbness; a daze
6. Ritual recitation of charms or spells to produce magic
7. Full of juice or sap; juicy
10. Caused great pain or anguish
11. Firm determination
12. Pride; joy
14. Cut into the surface of
15. Reproved gently but earnestly
17. Rendered motionless, as with terror or amazement
18. Unpleasantly sharp, pungent, or bitter to smell
19. A rut, groove, or narrow depression

Bless Me Ultima Vocabulary Juggle Letters 1

1. RYEESH = 1. _____
Dissension from dogma by a professed believer

2. OIPRDINET = 2. _____
Loss of soul; eternal damnation

3. ULOEINSTAYC = 3. _____
Persistently

4. CDFSOFE = 4. _____
Mocked or treated with derision

5. SAHTHES = 5. _____
Cases for sword or knife blades

6. TATANINCNIO = 6. _____
Ritual recitation of charms or spells to produce magic

7. NDEDEOW = 7. _____
Provided with property or income

8. ONRDEOC = 8. _____
Sung softly or in a humming way

9. MNAETDEA = 9. _____
Came forth or sent forth, as from a source

10. LIETONA = 10. _____
Pride; joy

11. IEATACDEM = 11. _____
Made extremely thin, especially as a result of starvation

12. RUKNGIL = 12. _____
Lying in wait, as in ambush

13. DCHETE = 13. _____
Cut into the surface of

14. OEDRUCNTE = 14. _____
Offered in response

15. LENEFTIG = 15. _____
Moving swiftly; rapid or nimble

Bless Me Ultima Vocabulary Juggle Letters 1 Answer Key

1. RYEESH = 1. HERESY
   Dissension from dogma by a professed believer

2. OIPRDINET = 2. PERDITION
   Loss of soul; eternal damnation

3. ULOEINSTAYC = 3. TENACIOUSLY
   Persistently

4. CDFSOFE = 4. SCOFFED
   Mocked or treated with derision

5. SAHTHES = 5. SHEATHS
   Cases for sword or knife blades

6. TATANINCNIO = 6. INCANTATION
   Ritual recitation of charms or spells to produce magic

7. NDEDEOW = 7. ENDOWED
   Provided with property or income

8. ONRDEOC = 8. CROONED
   Sung softly or in a humming way

9. MNAETDEA = 9. EMANATED
   Came forth or sent forth, as from a source

10. LIETONA = 10. ELATION
    Pride; joy

11. IEATACDEM = 11. EMACIATED
    Made extremely thin, especially as a result of starvation

12. RUKNGIL = 12. LURKING
    Lying in wait, as in ambush

13. DCHETE = 13. ETCHED
    Cut into the surface of

14. OEDRUCNTE = 14. COUNTERED
    Offered in response

15. LENEFTIG = 15. FLEETING
    Moving swiftly; rapid or nimble

Bless Me Ultima Vocabulary Juggle Letters 2

1. RDEON = 1. _____
   Continuous, low, dull humming sound

2. ITXSDRNFEA = 2. _____
   Rendered motionless, as with terror or amazement

3. BIRDSE = 3. _____
   Rubble or wreckage

4. DINIOTEPR = 4. _____
   Loss of soul; eternal damnation

5. TEEDYRYSN = 5. _____
   Inflammatory disorder of the lower intestinal tract

6. AUTEEBRNX = 6. _____
   Joyous; full of high spirits

7. YTILSLCOA = 7. _____
   Unaffected by pleasure or pain; impassively

8. ADDSEERCTE = 8. _____
   Violated the sacredness of; profaned

9. EDAROMCL = 9. _____
   Made a loud, sustained noise or outcry

10. LDIMENLUTIA = 10. _____
    Lit up

11. DTOMTNREE = 11. _____
    Caused great pain or anguish

12. HTSHSEA = 12. _____
    Cases for sword or knife blades

13. EDBITDNE = 13. _____
    Morally, socially, or legally obliged to another; beholden

14. EVDDLGUI = 14. _____
    Made known something private or secret

15. RDIAC = 15. _____
    Unpleasantly sharp, pungent, or bitter to smell

Bless Me Ultima Vocabulary Juggle Letters 2 Answer Key

1. RDEON = 1. DRONE
   Continuous, low, dull humming sound

2. ITXSDRNFEA = 2. TRANSFIXED
   Rendered motionless, as with terror or amazement

3. BIRDSE = 3. DEBRIS
   Rubble or wreckage

4. DINIOTEPR = 4. PERDITION
   Loss of soul; eternal damnation

5. TEEDYRYSN = 5. DYSENTERY
   Inflammatory disorder of the lower intestinal tract

6. AUTEEBRNX = 6. EXUBERANT
   Joyous; full of high spirits

7. YTILSLCOA = 7. STOICALLY
   Unaffected by pleasure or pain; impassively

8. ADDSEERCTE = 8. DESECRATED
   Violated the sacredness of; profaned

9. EDAROMCL = 9. CLAMORED
   Made a loud, sustained noise or outcry

10. LDIMENLUTIA = 10. ILLUMINATED
    Lit up

11. DTOMTNREE = 11. TORMENTED
    Caused great pain or anguish

12. HTSHSEA = 12. SHEATHS
    Cases for sword or knife blades

13. EDBITDNE = 13. INDEBTED
    Morally, socially, or legally obliged to another; beholden

14. EVDDLGUI = 14. DIVULGED
    Made known something private or secret

15. RDIAC = 15. ACRID
    Unpleasantly sharp, pungent, or bitter to smell

Bless Me Ultima Vocabulary Jugle Letters 3

1. UDESBDSI = 1. _____
   Became less agitated or active

2. EDNIPRITO = 2. _____
   Loss of soul; eternal damnation

3. IATCDEMEA = 3. _____
   Made extremely thin, especially as a result of starvation

4. WDNDOEE = 4. _____
   Provided with property or income

5. UWORFR = 5. _____
   A rut, groove, or narrow depression

6. OLITSERUNO = 6. _____
   Firm determination

7. GAOBNSDAV = 7. _____
   People without permanent homes

8. ETCDEH = 8. _____
   Cut into the surface of

9. ENREUCDOT = 9. _____
   Offered in response

10. TOMES = 10. _____
    Very small particles; specks

11. LPAIUEDNTMA = 11. _____
    Influenced or managed shrewdly or deviously

12. OTALEIN = 12. _____
    Pride; joy

13. EDAECSDERT = 13. _____
    Violated the sacredness of; profaned

14. UTXNRBEEA = 14. _____
    Joyous; full of high spirits

15. SDETEYRNY = 15. _____
    Inflammatory disorder of the lower intestinal tract

Bless Me Ultima Vocabulary Juggle Letters 3 Answer Key

1. UDESBDSI = 1. SUBSIDED
   Became less agitated or active

2. EDNIPRITO = 2. PERDITION
   Loss of soul; eternal damnation

3. IATCDEMEA = 3. EMACIATED
   Made extremely thin, especially as a result of starvation

4. WDNDOEE = 4. ENDOWED
   Provided with property or income

5. UWORFR = 5. FURROW
   A rut, groove, or narrow depression

6. OLITSERUNO = 6. RESOLUTION
   Firm determination

7. GAOBNSDAV = 7. VAGABONDS
   People without permanent homes

8. ETCDEH = 8. ETCHED
   Cut into the surface of

9. ENREUCDOT = 9. COUNTERED
   Offered in response

10. TOMES = 10. MOTES
    Very small particles; specks

11. LPAIUEDNTMA = 11. MANIPULATED
    Influenced or managed shrewdly or deviously

12. OTALEIN = 12. ELATION
    Pride; joy

13. EDAECSDERT = 13. DESECRATED
    Violated the sacredness of; profaned

14. UTXNRBEEA = 14. EXUBERANT
    Joyous; full of high spirits

15. SDETEYRNY = 15. DYSENTERY
    Inflammatory disorder of the lower intestinal tract

Bless Me Ultima Vocabulary Juggle Letters 4

1. ATEIECMAD = 1. _____
   Made extremely thin, especially as a result of starvation

2. DERVAQUE = 2. _____
   Trembled

3. ENRUBTDEUPR = 3. _____
   Not disturbed or confused

4. UCTAIDYA = 4. _____
   Fearlessness; boldness

5. GPEINNMDI = 5. _____
   About to take place

6. VNARCAA = 6. _____
   Company of travelers journeying together

7. EBRIDSTL = 7. _____
   Caused to stand erect; stiffened

8. USIRTNNOI = 8. _____
   Rude or inappropriate entrance

9. INOCMTOOM = 9. _____
   Agitated disturbance

10. HSHSATE = 10. _____
    Cases for sword or knife blades

11. GSDOVNBAA = 11. _____
    People without permanent homes

12. URLOITNSEO = 12. _____
    Firm determination

13. WNDEEOD = 13. _____
    Provided with property or income

14. YYDRSETEN = 14. _____
    Inflammatory disorder of the lower intestinal tract

15. NEITIPODR = 15. _____
    Loss of soul; eternal damnation

Bless Me Ultima Vocabulary Juggle Letters 4 Answer Key

1. ATEIECMAD = 1. EMACIATED
   Made extremely thin, especially as a result of starvation

2. DERVAQUE = 2. QUAVERED
   Trembled

3. ENRUBTDEUPR = 3. UNPERTURBED
   Not disturbed or confused

4. UCTAIDYA = 4. AUDACITY
   Fearlessness; boldness

5. GPEINNMDI = 5. IMPENDING
   About to take place

6. VNARCAA = 6. CARAVAN
   Company of travelers journeying together

7. EBRIDSTL = 7. BRISTLED
   Caused to stand erect; stiffened

8. USIRTNNOI = 8. INTRUSION
   Rude or inappropriate entrance

9. INOCMTOOM = 9. COMMOTION
   Agitated disturbance

10. HSHSATE = 10. SHEATHS
    Cases for sword or knife blades

11. GSDOVNBAA = 11. VAGABONDS
    People without permanent homes

12. URLOITNSEO = 12. RESOLUTION
    Firm determination

13. WNDEEOD = 13. ENDOWED
    Provided with property or income

14. YYDRSETEN = 14. DYSENTERY
    Inflammatory disorder of the lower intestinal tract

15. NEITIPODR = 15. PERDITION
    Loss of soul; eternal damnation

ABRUPTLY	Suddenly
ACRID	Unpleasantly sharp, pungent, or bitter to smell
ADMONISHED	Reproved gently but earnestly
ARROGANT	Making claims to unwarranted importance
AUDACITY	Fearlessness; boldness
BLEMISH	Imperfection that mars or impairs

BRISTLED	Caused to stand erect; stiffened
CARAVAN	Company of travelers journeying together
CLAMORED	Made a loud, sustained noise or outcry
COMMOTION	Agitated disturbance
CONTEMPTUOUSLY	Disdainfully; scornfully
COUNTERED	Offered in response

CROONED	Sung softly or in a humming way
DEBRIS	Rubble or wreckage
DEFIANCE	Bold resistance
DESECRATED	Violated the sacredness of; profaned
DISQUIETUDE	Worried unease; anxiety
DIVULGED	Made known something private or secret

DRONE	Continuous, low, dull humming sound
DYSENTERY	Inflammatory disorder of the lower intestinal tract
ELATION	Pride; joy
EMACIATED	Made extremely thin, especially as a result of starvation
EMANATED	Came forth or sent forth, as from a source
EMPHATICALLY	Positively; definitely

ENDOWED	Provided with property or income
ENDURES	Continues in existence; lasts
ETCHED	Cut into the surface of
EXASPERATION	Anger or impatience
EXORCISE	Free from evil spirits or malign influences
EXUBERANT	Joyous; full of high spirits

FLEETING	Moving swiftly; rapid or nimble
FORAGE	Wander in search of food or provisions
FORSAKING	Giving up something formerly held dear
FURROW	A rut, groove, or narrow depression
HERESY	Dissension from dogma by a professed believer
ILLUMINATED	Lit up

IMPENDING	About to take place
INCANTATION	Ritual recitation of charms or spells to produce magic
INDEBTED	Morally, socially, or legally obliged to another; beholden
INSTINCTIVELY	Done by innate aptitude
INTERMINABLE	Endless
INTRUSION	Rude or inappropriate entrance

IRREVOCABLE	Impossible to retract or take back
LURKING	Lying in wait, as in ambush
MANIPULATED	Influenced or managed shrewdly or deviously
MELEE	Violent free-for-all
MOTES	Very small particles; specks
OBSTACLES	Things that oppose or stand in the way of

PERDITION	Loss of soul; eternal damnation
PHANTOMS	Ghosts or apparitions
PULSATING	Expanding and contracting rhythmically; beating
QUAVERED	Trembled
RESIGNED	Unresistingly accepting
RESOLUTION	Firm determination

REVERBERATING	Resounding in a series of echoes
SARDONICALLY	Scornfully or cynically mocking
SCOFFED	Mocked or treated with derision
SHEATHS	Cases for sword or knife blades
STOICALLY	Unaffected by pleasure or pain; impassively
STUPOR	State of mental numbness; a daze

SUBSIDED	Became less agitated or active
SUCCULENT	Full of juice or sap; juicy
TENACIOUSLY	Persistently
TORMENTED	Caused great pain or anguish
TRANSFIXED	Rendered motionless, as with terror or amazement
UNPERTURBED	Not disturbed or confused

VAGABONDS	People without permanent homes
VIGILANTES	Those who take law enforcement upon themselves
WROUGHT	Created; put together

Bless Me Ultima Vocabulary

COMMOTION	DEFIANCE	PULSATING	ELATION	BLEMISH
ILLUMINATED	CLAMORED	IRREVOCABLE	QUAVERED	ACRID
DYSENTERY	ENDOWED	FREE SPACE	PERDITION	SUBSIDED
IMPENDING	EXORCISE	WROUGHT	LURKING	EMACIATED
EMANATED	ENDURES	INSTINCTIVELY	RESOLUTION	ETCHED

Bless Me Ultima Vocabulary

PHANTOMS	INTRUSION	REVERBERATING	ADMONISHED	SHEATHS
DISQUIETUDE	RESIGNED	DEBRIS	FORSAKING	TORMENTED
DESECRATED	ABRUPTLY	FREE SPACE	SARDONICALLY	CROONED
FURROW	INDEBTED	INTERMINABLE	SCOFFED	STOICALLY
DRONE	FLEETING	COUNTERED	MELEE	VAGABONDS

Bless Me Ultima Vocabulary

OBSTACLES	PULSATING	TRANSFIXED	FORAGE	RESOLUTION
AUDACITY	VIGILANTES	CROONED	DEBRIS	IRREVOCABLE
PHANTOMS	ACRID	FREE SPACE	EXASPERATION	INTRUSION
FLEETING	MOTES	BRISTLED	MANIPULATED	SCOFFED
CARAVAN	ENDURES	EMANATED	INCANTATION	EMPHATICALLY

Bless Me Ultima Vocabulary

REVERBERATING	UNPERTURBED	FURROW	DESECRATED	DEFIANCE
MELEE	LURKING	INDEBTED	QUAVERED	STUPOR
SARDONICALLY	TENACIOUSLY	FREE SPACE	INSTINCTIVELY	TORMENTED
FORSAKING	INTERMINABLE	EXUBERANT	PERDITION	ILLUMINATED
COUNTERED	DYSENTERY	COMMOTION	SUCCULENT	SHEATHS

Bless Me Ultima Vocabulary

LURKING	ILLUMINATED	IRREVOCABLE	REVERBERATING	INSTINCTIVELY
SCOFFED	ADMONISHED	PERDITION	AUDACITY	PHANTOMS
VIGILANTES	ENDURES	FREE SPACE	BRISTLED	WROUGHT
QUAVERED	INTRUSION	MOTES	SUBSIDED	OBSTACLES
SHEATHS	ACRID	RESOLUTION	PULSATING	ETCHED

Bless Me Ultima Vocabulary

INDEBTED	EXORCISE	HERESY	CLAMORED	FURROW
INTERMINABLE	SUCCULENT	RESIGNED	INCANTATION	CROONED
CONTEMPTUOUSLY	BLEMISH	FREE SPACE	SARDONICALLY	UNPERTURBED
ABRUPTLY	STOICALLY	DEFIANCE	MELEE	STUPOR
FORAGE	COUNTERED	EMPHATICALLY	ENDOWED	ARROGANT

Bless Me Ultima Vocabulary

SCOFFED	INDEBTED	DYSENTERY	DISQUIETUDE	LURKING
DEBRIS	DESECRATED	INTERMINABLE	INTRUSION	EMANATED
TENACIOUSLY	EMACIATED	FREE SPACE	RESOLUTION	AUDACITY
STOICALLY	COMMOTION	WROUGHT	QUAVERED	EXUBERANT
FORAGE	ABRUPTLY	VAGABONDS	BRISTLED	ETCHED

Bless Me Ultima Vocabulary

IMPENDING	OBSTACLES	SARDONICALLY	STUPOR	TRANSFIXED
ELATION	BLEMISH	RESIGNED	ARROGANT	MOTES
FURROW	FLEETING	FREE SPACE	TORMENTED	HERESY
INCANTATION	REVERBERATING	EXASPERATION	CLAMORED	ENDOWED
DRONE	COUNTERED	MANIPULATED	ENDURES	INSTINCTIVELY

Bless Me Ultima Vocabulary

TRANSFIXED	SUBSIDED	ARROGANT	EXUBERANT	EMACIATED
INTRUSION	BRISTLED	INTERMINABLE	INCANTATION	IMPENDING
PULSATING	CLAMORED	FREE SPACE	ETCHED	INDEBTED
LURKING	IRREVOCABLE	ENDURES	ELATION	EMPHATICALLY
DEFIANCE	CARAVAN	ABRUPTLY	INSTINCTIVELY	PERDITION

Bless Me Ultima Vocabulary

VAGABONDS	FORSAKING	ENDOWED	RESIGNED	FORAGE
UNPERTURBED	HERESY	TENACIOUSLY	QUAVERED	ILLUMINATED
BLEMISH	SHEATHS	FREE SPACE	COMMOTION	DISQUIETUDE
EMANATED	DRONE	DYSENTERY	CROONED	DEBRIS
WROUGHT	OBSTACLES	MELEE	ADMONISHED	MOTES

Bless Me Ultima Vocabulary

ABRUPTLY	AUDACITY	INTERMINABLE	DESECRATED	DEBRIS
RESOLUTION	RESIGNED	TENACIOUSLY	PHANTOMS	BLEMISH
EXUBERANT	ARROGANT	FREE SPACE	BRISTLED	TRANSFIXED
SUBSIDED	MELEE	COUNTERED	FORSAKING	ACRID
SARDONICALLY	ENDURES	INSTINCTIVELY	COMMOTION	ETCHED

Bless Me Ultima Vocabulary

DRONE	VIGILANTES	CROONED	INCANTATION	CLAMORED
MANIPULATED	INTRUSION	MOTES	DISQUIETUDE	STOICALLY
STUPOR	PERDITION	FREE SPACE	VAGABONDS	ILLUMINATED
EXASPERATION	FURROW	FLEETING	QUAVERED	SCOFFED
CARAVAN	OBSTACLES	IMPENDING	DIVULGED	IRREVOCABLE

Bless Me Ultima Vocabulary

SUCCULENT	ELATION	OBSTACLES	ENDOWED	STUPOR
BLEMISH	VAGABONDS	ARROGANT	REVERBERATING	DESECRATED
CLAMORED	DISQUIETUDE	FREE SPACE	EXASPERATION	EMANATED
WROUGHT	PHANTOMS	ILLUMINATED	QUAVERED	RESOLUTION
DEBRIS	SCOFFED	INCANTATION	SHEATHS	FURROW

Bless Me Ultima Vocabulary

CARAVAN	ACRID	TORMENTED	VIGILANTES	EXUBERANT
INSTINCTIVELY	MELEE	ADMONISHED	DIVULGED	AUDACITY
MANIPULATED	LURKING	FREE SPACE	INTRUSION	CROONED
COMMOTION	FORSAKING	ENDURES	INTERMINABLE	STOICALLY
SARDONICALLY	ETCHED	UNPERTURBED	ABRUPTLY	DEFIANCE

Bless Me Ultima Vocabulary

TORMENTED	RESOLUTION	IRREVOCABLE	FORSAKING	PULSATING
MELEE	AUDACITY	WROUGHT	PERDITION	SUBSIDED
COMMOTION	VAGABONDS	FREE SPACE	INTERMINABLE	VIGILANTES
MOTES	SUCCULENT	UNPERTURBED	QUAVERED	ENDOWED
FORAGE	ACRID	DYSENTERY	ARROGANT	SARDONICALLY

Bless Me Ultima Vocabulary

EXORCISE	DESECRATED	FLEETING	FURROW	EMACIATED
ELATION	DISQUIETUDE	DIVULGED	CARAVAN	CONTEMPTUOUSLY
SHEATHS	EMANATED	FREE SPACE	EXASPERATION	CROONED
INDEBTED	ABRUPTLY	SCOFFED	TENACIOUSLY	REVERBERATING
CLAMORED	DRONE	OBSTACLES	INTRUSION	ENDURES

Bless Me Ultima Vocabulary

ABRUPTLY	STUPOR	BLEMISH	TRANSFIXED	CARAVAN
QUAVERED	FURROW	INTERMINABLE	COUNTERED	ARROGANT
EMANATED	DYSENTERY	FREE SPACE	IRREVOCABLE	FLEETING
DISQUIETUDE	MANIPULATED	COMMOTION	PHANTOMS	REVERBERATING
EXASPERATION	EMACIATED	HERESY	CROONED	ACRID

Bless Me Ultima Vocabulary

CLAMORED	MOTES	WROUGHT	ILLUMINATED	TORMENTED
DIVULGED	LURKING	SARDONICALLY	SUBSIDED	INSTINCTIVELY
SUCCULENT	FORSAKING	FREE SPACE	EMPHATICALLY	INCANTATION
INTRUSION	AUDACITY	INDEBTED	DESECRATED	EXUBERANT
MELEE	CONTEMPTUOUSLY	FORAGE	OBSTACLES	EXORCISE

Bless Me Ultima Vocabulary

SARDONICALLY	IRREVOCABLE	MOTES	TENACIOUSLY	PULSATING
EXUBERANT	ENDURES	DESECRATED	EXORCISE	COMMOTION
ENDOWED	ARROGANT	FREE SPACE	RESIGNED	SHEATHS
OBSTACLES	COUNTERED	EMACIATED	INSTINCTIVELY	VAGABONDS
SUCCULENT	STOICALLY	MANIPULATED	REVERBERATING	UNPERTURBED

Bless Me Ultima Vocabulary

EMANATED	ABRUPTLY	SUBSIDED	TRANSFIXED	CONTEMPTUOUSLY
ELATION	QUAVERED	VIGILANTES	DEFIANCE	EXASPERATION
CARAVAN	EMPHATICALLY	FREE SPACE	FORAGE	AUDACITY
DRONE	IMPENDING	TORMENTED	ETCHED	BLEMISH
ADMONISHED	WROUGHT	INCANTATION	INTRUSION	STUPOR

Bless Me Ultima Vocabulary

ACRID	VAGABONDS	PHANTOMS	BRISTLED	TENACIOUSLY
TRANSFIXED	REVERBERATING	INTERMINABLE	SARDONICALLY	EMANATED
STUPOR	CROONED	FREE SPACE	ETCHED	DRONE
TORMENTED	LURKING	DEBRIS	DISQUIETUDE	STOICALLY
DESECRATED	COMMOTION	FLEETING	CONTEMPTUOUSLY	WROUGHT

Bless Me Ultima Vocabulary

FURROW	COUNTERED	RESOLUTION	MANIPULATED	DIVULGED
SCOFFED	OBSTACLES	EXUBERANT	MELEE	SUBSIDED
ELATION	INDEBTED	FREE SPACE	EXASPERATION	DEFIANCE
ADMONISHED	PULSATING	DYSENTERY	INTRUSION	ARROGANT
EXORCISE	ABRUPTLY	IRREVOCABLE	ENDOWED	CARAVAN

Bless Me Ultima Vocabulary

OBSTACLES	SCOFFED	ACRID	TORMENTED	WROUGHT
SARDONICALLY	STOICALLY	TRANSFIXED	REVERBERATING	EXORCISE
IRREVOCABLE	IMPENDING	FREE SPACE	RESOLUTION	SUBSIDED
CROONED	ETCHED	SUCCULENT	LURKING	ELATION
DYSENTERY	VAGABONDS	INTRUSION	HERESY	UNPERTURBED

Bless Me Ultima Vocabulary

PHANTOMS	DISQUIETUDE	EXASPERATION	DESECRATED	ADMONISHED
DEFIANCE	TENACIOUSLY	DEBRIS	FURROW	EMANATED
INDEBTED	VIGILANTES	FREE SPACE	MANIPULATED	ENDURES
ARROGANT	EMPHATICALLY	QUAVERED	FORSAKING	DIVULGED
CARAVAN	EMACIATED	ABRUPTLY	BLEMISH	INCANTATION

Bless Me Ultima Vocabulary

EXORCISE	VIGILANTES	HERESY	SHEATHS	ILLUMINATED
BRISTLED	PULSATING	DYSENTERY	FURROW	COMMOTION
MANIPULATED	EXUBERANT	FREE SPACE	OBSTACLES	CONTEMPTUOUSLY
ENDURES	BLEMISH	DESECRATED	INDEBTED	REVERBERATING
AUDACITY	INTERMINABLE	DEFIANCE	FLEETING	RESOLUTION

Bless Me Ultima Vocabulary

INCANTATION	FORSAKING	INTRUSION	DEBRIS	CLAMORED
SUBSIDED	COUNTERED	UNPERTURBED	MOTES	TENACIOUSLY
QUAVERED	TORMENTED	FREE SPACE	ACRID	EXASPERATION
ADMONISHED	ARROGANT	LURKING	IMPENDING	EMPHATICALLY
SCOFFED	PHANTOMS	STUPOR	CARAVAN	SARDONICALLY

Bless Me Ultima Vocabulary

CLAMORED	SUCCULENT	MOTES	CONTEMPTUOUSLY	TRANSFIXED
ILLUMINATED	LURKING	BRISTLED	DEFIANCE	ARROGANT
QUAVERED	DEBRIS	FREE SPACE	EMPHATICALLY	ACRID
CROONED	PERDITION	EMANATED	PULSATING	COMMOTION
SUBSIDED	TENACIOUSLY	BLEMISH	INSTINCTIVELY	ELATION

Bless Me Ultima Vocabulary

DYSENTERY	REVERBERATING	OBSTACLES	ENDURES	MANIPULATED
EMACIATED	ADMONISHED	ETCHED	COUNTERED	MELEE
HERESY	INDEBTED	FREE SPACE	AUDACITY	ABRUPTLY
DISQUIETUDE	DRONE	INTRUSION	EXASPERATION	FLEETING
FORAGE	WROUGHT	IRREVOCABLE	INTERMINABLE	SHEATHS

Bless Me Ultima Vocabulary

FLEETING	EXUBERANT	INTRUSION	SUCCULENT	IMPENDING
RESOLUTION	REVERBERATING	SUBSIDED	SCOFFED	ABRUPTLY
ACRID	TRANSFIXED	FREE SPACE	DRONE	SARDONICALLY
ILLUMINATED	PHANTOMS	COUNTERED	WROUGHT	DISQUIETUDE
ELATION	PULSATING	STUPOR	MANIPULATED	ETCHED

Bless Me Ultima Vocabulary

HERESY	ADMONISHED	INTERMINABLE	ENDURES	EMANATED
TORMENTED	INCANTATION	IRREVOCABLE	LURKING	CONTEMPTUOUSLY
MOTES	CARAVAN	FREE SPACE	EXASPERATION	TENACIOUSLY
STOICALLY	FORAGE	INDEBTED	COMMOTION	EXORCISE
ARROGANT	BLEMISH	SHEATHS	EMACIATED	AUDACITY

Bless Me Ultima Vocabulary

CONTEMPTUOUSLY	IMPENDING	ILLUMINATED	ENDURES	COMMOTION
SUCCULENT	DIVULGED	IRREVOCABLE	CLAMORED	HERESY
TENACIOUSLY	QUAVERED	FREE SPACE	FORSAKING	PERDITION
EXASPERATION	ETCHED	ADMONISHED	SHEATHS	INTRUSION
TRANSFIXED	REVERBERATING	DEBRIS	EMACIATED	RESOLUTION

Bless Me Ultima Vocabulary

SARDONICALLY	INSTINCTIVELY	EMPHATICALLY	UNPERTURBED	CARAVAN
DRONE	VIGILANTES	FORAGE	MOTES	AUDACITY
CROONED	DESECRATED	FREE SPACE	BRISTLED	EXUBERANT
MANIPULATED	INDEBTED	DYSENTERY	EXORCISE	ACRID
DEFIANCE	SCOFFED	PULSATING	ENDOWED	WROUGHT

www.ingramcontent.com/pod-product-compliance
Lightning Source LLC
Chambersburg PA
CBHW081453070526
44586CB00019B/2336